BUY

THE

FIELD

Find, Follow, and Finish God's Call for Your Life

ROB FLESHMAN

First published in 2016 by Striving Together Publications, a
ministry of Lancaster Baptist Church, Lancaster, CA 93535.
Striving Together Publications is committed to providing
tried, trusted, and proven books that will further equip local
churches to carry out the Great Commission. Your comments
and suggestions are valued.

Striving Together Publications
4020 E. Lancaster Blvd.
Lancaster, CA 93535
800.201.7748

Cover design by Andrew Jones
Layout by Craig Parker
Special thanks to our proofreaders

The author and publication team have put forth every effort to give
proper credit to quotes and thoughts that are not original with the
author. It is not our intent to claim originality with any quote or
thought that could not readily be tied to an original source.

ISBN 978-1-59894-319-1

Printed in the United States of America

This book is dedicated to the love of my life, Michelle. Who, for more than 20 years of marriage, has never yielded to any such temptation to quit or turn back on the field of marriage she bought on a cold winter's day in December of 1991.

Thank you for being a faithful source of inspiration and courage for me, our four children, and all those who long to find, follow, and finish God's call for their life.

There are two sayings that I borrowed many years ago that still resonate in my heart: "You measure greatness by what it takes to stop you," and "how can you stop a man who will not quit?". I think of those two sayings afresh, when I read Rob Fleshman's book. This great reading will challenge you to be time conscious and goal oriented making very sure that you live out your life to its fullest potential, and be able to hear from the Lord, "Well done…" thus assuring that you did what you were supposed to do, while in your field.

—**Dr. Max Alderman, Evangelist, Statesboro, Georgia**

Finding your field! As a pastor at the same church for a long time, I have seen the frustration in fellow Christians' lives as they struggle to find their cause or place in the work of God. In this book, Pastor Fleshman does a phenomenal job of helping everyone see that there is a field just for you and that God has you picked out for such a field! I strongly endorse this book! Read it, live it, and Buy Your Field!

—**Dr. Randy Dignan, Pastor of Bible Baptist Church in Jefferson City, Missouri, home to Listening Heart Ministries**

What a tremendous resource this book is. Rob Fleshman's *Buy the Field* is a thoroughly unique and important volume in many ways. I am certain that it will be used as a ministry tool often in Bible-centered churches. The uniqueness of this book is found in its thorough, in-depth Bible study on the matter of one discerning God's plan for his life. Yet it doesn't stop with simply the discernment of God's will; it takes you on the journey of discovering the joys and utter benefits of fulfilling God's plan for your life. It will also serve as a tool to encourage one to simply stay faithful to accomplish God's plan when times get turbulent, and it appears that not much fruit is being borne in your personal field. I am constantly on the lookout for good books for thoughtful students about the issues of Christian living. *Buy The Field* is one I can whole-heartedly recommend for any serious disciple of Christ.

—**Morris Gleiser, Evangelist, Indianapolis, Indiana and Author, *The Journey: Navigating your Teenage Years***

How to know God's will is a question often asked. As a pastor, after giving Biblical counsel, I will sometimes follow it up with recommending a specific book to read on the subject. When it comes to knowing and doing God's will, Pastor Fleshman's book is one of highest recommendation.

—**Steve Henderson, Pastor, Harvest Baptist Church, Manhattan, Kansas**

Reading a spiritual book should inspire change and cause one to stand in awe at the greatness of God and the clear teaching He has delivered through His word. Pastor Fleshman has done this by focusing on a very consuming subject for every believer. If one doesn't find and follow God's purpose for life then they have missed what life is all about! The uniquely interwoven illustration of *Buy the Field* is a masterful and meaningful way of portraying this powerful truth. The personal touch and thought provoking material of both biblical and illustrated truth is a perfect blend. Rob's writing style is easy and pleasing to read and deeply focused on the heart. This book will no doubt challenge you, convict and correct you, comfort you, and change you to pursue the most profitable existence you can have. If you are seeking to grow in Christ and to walk in the "good and acceptable and perfect will of God" then *Buy the Field* is a must read!

—**Mike Herbster, Evangelist and Director of Southland Christian Camp in Ringgold, Louisiana**

Buy the Field is a book that is long overdue. It is truly a "faith can move mountains" kind of book. He offers up one challenge after another as it relates to the "field of **your** dreams." I told him when I read it, "I wish I had written this book" in conjunction with my message on "A Treasure hid in a field." It's a book every preacher should read and a must for preachers just starting out. I highly recommend it.

**—Dr. Lawrence D. Hufhand, Editor of the Hufhand Report
and retired Pastor**

I am thankful for the resolve of Pastor Fleshman to write a book that can be of practical help to our Independent Baptist Churches. I appreciate the insight that *Buy the Field* offers into Bible truth and Rob Fleshman's ability to illustrate, making it easier for the reader to make application. You will be confronted with the reality that God has a definite plan for your life and convicted by His requirement of stewardship over this life, yet at the same time encouraged by the powerful provision that God has made available!

**—Billy Ingram, Pastor, Canaan Baptist Church,
Covington, Georgia**

Wow! What a resource. Rob Fleshman does a great job of seamlessly intertwining biblical truths with excellent illustrations. This is a book that will challenge you to take seriously the call of God on your life. Although this book is a great help to pastors, its scope and impact should not be limited to just those in vocational ministry. The simple fact is that God has a call on your life. There is a unique place of service for every child of God. Pastor Fleshman does a great job of drawing word pictures which help enrich our vision and warm our hearts for the calling of God on your lives. I found this easy-to-read book strengthening my resolve as it described the "ups and downs" of living for Christ and the incredible privilege it is to have a part in God's plan. Finding, following, and finishing God's call on our lives is the key to living a life with *no regrets*. As each biblical truth is layered upon the previous, the evidence starts to become insurmountable and the author leaves us with but one conclusion— buy the field! The field is not cheap, but it is worth every penny.

> **—Chris Myers, Pastor, First Baptist Church, Irondale, Missouri**

Buy the Field is written to motivate you to act in faith to what God wants to do in your life for His glory. It is a call to action. If you are interested in serving Christ and being motivated, act now, buy the field, and read this book. It will send you on your way to buying more fields.

> **—Stan Templeton, Church Planting Missionary in Peru**

A successful life, versus a life of disappointment and failure, can be determined by finding the will of God for one's life and doing it. Rob Fleshman has written an excellent book on this subject that is a pleasure to read, as his manuscript contrasts the Biblical view of a life and the secular approach to it. If everyone in our city or town knew, believed, and lived according to the truths of this writing, we would have a sanctuary.

> **—Dr. Tom Wallace, Evangelist and Pastor Emeritus of Franklin Road Baptist Church in Murfreesboro, Tennessee**

CONTENTS

PREFACE

*Again, the kingdom of heaven is like unto treasure hid
in a field; the which when a man hath found, he hideth,
and for joy thereof goeth and selleth all that he hath, and
buyeth that field.*—Matthew 13:44

The field filled with treasure still calls to mankind, luring him in with its promise of wealth. Hundreds of artists etch onto canvas enduring, picturesque images of their favorite views. Musicians sing of the strawberry variety. Developers build on them, lovers go for long strolls in them, farmers intensively labor in them, and realtors do their best to buy and sell them. Whatever part of the country we call home, from baseball to cotton, wheat to soccer, and football to pumpkins, we are inescapably surrounded by fields.

But despite sharing a common name, this book concerns itself with none of such fields. Rather, I write to encourage you to find, follow, and finish your calling in your field. I refer to that acutely personal, high calling of God that is part of

His plan for the lives of every one of His children. Perhaps for you it is the construction field. For another it is the education field. For still others it may be the nursing field, mechanics field, youth ministry field, the culinary arts field, or hundreds of other such fields. Whatever your God-appointed field, may the biblical precepts presented in the following pages serve to inspire you to buy the field, work your field, and stay in your field for the cause of Christ.

THE ORIGINAL BRIDGE
TO NOWHERE

In the 1970s, construction was underway on the Olimpijka, a planned east-west 310-mile-long motorway across the country of Poland that linked highway infrastructure between Berlin and Moscow. While originally expected to open in time for the 1980 Summer Olympic Games held in Moscow, gripping economic times, as well as a tumultuous political landscape and ever-shifting national priorities, led to the halting of construction and the eventual abandonment of the Olimpijka project.

All that was left of the planning, time, and effort was a single thirty-one mile section of the highway, completed and opened for use in the 1980s. In the final analysis, though, only 10 percent of the 310-mile-long dream actually came to fruition. The remainder is a vagabond collection of ruins. A field lined with forty or fifty concrete support pillars, intended to undergird the highway, now stands isolated, supporting only the nests of birds on its sturdy frame. A meadow lined with trees, piles of dirt here, a graffiti-stained aqueduct there, and a most curious 100-foot-long isolated section of a concrete viaduct proudly resting on pillars jutting thirty feet in the air. Apparently, plans were for this last portion to be an overpass when it grew up, but alas, the stand-alone structure comes from out of nowhere and serves as a bridge to nowhere as well.

The 100 percent planned but 90 percent unfinished Olimpijka bears a striking resemblance to the modern-day dreams and life pursuits of many Christians. Carefully wished-upon plans never materialize and leave behind fragments of ruin as a testimony to what might have been. Chalk it up to a myriad of causes: a financial crunch, a failed relationship, a family to raise, a bad health report from the doctor, or even a mid-life crisis that starts long before and runs well past midlife. The excuses are numerous, and the end results are predictable: Olimpijka.

(Similarly, it has been estimated that in Bible times, the Israelites only conquered about 10 percent of the land that God had in store for His people. That's about the same percentage as what project Olimpijka managed to check off as done in the 1980s, and 10 percent is probably dangerously close to that which the average Christian today realizes of all the plans that God has in store for him.)

It turns out that the forever-to-remain unfinished Olimpijka roadway was slated to be built over a planned, but also unfinished, motorway that Nazi Germany began after their invasion of Poland. And as another illustration of history repeating itself, the blueprints for the A2 motorway (begun in 2010) call for it to be built right over the top of (you guessed it) what would have been Olimpijka. Any and all remnants of Olimpijka are scheduled to be torn down and destroyed as part of construction of the A2.

Better pick up the pace and blow the dust off your well-intended plans, and the blueprints of your life's dream. The heavy earth moving equipment of time and neglect are seen rolling in from the distance and the bulldozers of regret and missed opportunities are about to fire up their engines.

PART ONE
FIND GOD'S CALL

Believe with all of your heart that you will do what you were made to do.—**Orison Swett Marden**

Decision and determination are the engineer and fireman of our train to opportunity and success.—**Burt Lawlor**

In a free society, every opportunity comes with three obligations. First, you must seize it. You must mold it into a work that brings value to others. Second, you must live it. Opportunity is nurtured only by action. Third, you must defend the freedom to pursue opportunities….—**Robert C. Goizueta**

Twenty years from now you will be more disappointed by the things you didn't do than by the ones you did do. So throw off the bowlines. Sail away from the safe harbor. Catch the trade winds in your sails. Explore. Dream. Discover.—**Mark Twain**

CHAPTER ONE

YOU HAVE A FIELD

Let thine eyes be on the field...—RUTH 2:9

A favorite children's song sung in Sunday Schools and Vacation Bible Schools is as follows:

> O, be careful little eyes what you see.
> O, be careful little eyes what you see.
> For the Father up above
> Is looking down in love,
> So be careful little eyes what you see.

This short melody's verses offer up the same cautionary challenge to one's ears, tongue, mind, hands, and feet. The emphasis is on the tongue not saying wrong things or the feet not going to wrong places and so forth. Doing, speaking, hearing, thinking, going, and seeing things which we ought not is what we call "sins of commission"—that is, committing those acts of sin that are contrary to the teachings of Scripture.

But there is another manner of sin equally offensive to a Holy God that routinely flies well below the radar in the life of the busy Christian. I am not referring to the committing of wrong things, but rather to the omitting of right things. James 4:17 warns, *"Therefore to him that knoweth to do good, and doeth it not, to him it is sin."* These good deeds left undone are classified as sins of omission. Equally repugnant, but receiving far less press, these iniquities involve unwisely leaving undone the doing, saying, or thinking of right things which we know ought to be done, said, or thought.

> *Finally, brethren, whatsoever things are true, whatsoever things are honest, whatsoever things are just, whatsoever things are pure, whatsoever things are lovely, whatsoever things are of good report; if there be any virtue, and if there be any praise, think on these things. Those things, which ye have both learned, and received, and heard, and seen in me, do: and the God of peace shall be with you.*—PHILIPPIANS 4:8–9

Pure things could involve sharing the gospel with others; just things could mean giving our best to God; and true things could include letting our mind's eye be on the field, as Boaz admonished Ruth: *"Let thine eyes be on the field that they do reap, and go thou after them"* (Ruth 2:9). Ruth needed food and water. Boaz was aware of Ruth's predicament and had provisions in place for meeting her every need and much more. But for those provisions to journey from his hand to hers, the command of obedience meant that Ruth's eyes *"be on the field."* The reason for this command was that Boaz, the Kinsman-Redeemer and a type of the Lord Jesus Christ, not only had a plan to meet her need but also had a place. The place was a specific field where that plan was to be fulfilled. If Ruth's eyes were affixed anywhere other than the field she was directed toward, then the plan would not be accomplished, at least not as God had intended, and she would unnecessarily lack and suffer.

EARS, OPEN. EYEBALLS, CLICK.

Whether we give credence to the notion or not, children are protégés—apprentices to life—in more ways than adults often take the time to consider. God has implanted within impressionable young minds a great capacity to learn, and such learning is best assimilated through modeling the mannerisms of their mentors, including parents, teachers, pastors, and other authority figures in their lives. However, this assimilation of learning through mentorship is a two-edged sword. While helpful traits that serve to enable await their inheritance, so do hindering habits which exist only to cripple.

One such crippling habit is a lack of godly focus. A life marked by great achievement for God is the byproduct of a life of great focus and singularity to please the Lord. Paul knew the unbridled power of a Christ-focused, surrendered life when, under the inspiration of the Holy Spirit, he wrote, *"Brethren, I count not myself to have apprehended: but this one thing I do, forgetting those things which are behind, and reaching forth unto those things which are before, I press toward the mark for the prize of the high calling of God in Christ Jesus"* (Philippians 3:13–14).

Satan also knows this, and he is relentless in his base work of distraction and untiring in his sinister attempts to keep the eyes of Christians off God and out of focus with His will for their lives. In such times, we unwittingly yield to subtle temptations again and again. What is the biblical antidote when we find ourselves entrenched in the abysmal mire of a clouded, distracted life? Simply this: purposeful, highly intentional living powered by focus.

Referring to focus in the area of business, J. Paul Getty once said: "The individual who wants to reach the top in business must appreciate the might of the force of habit—and must understand that practices are what create habits. He must be quick to break those habits that can break him—and hasten to adopt those practices that will become the habits that help him achieve the success he desires."

One exercise for teachers to regain the lost attention and focus of their pupils is, *"Ears, open! Eyeballs, click!"* (I am told that it is also a tried-and-true tool for Marine Corps drill instructors.) When children's minds are in a aimless state of meandering and inattention, the teacher may shout out, *"Ears!"* The response expected from the class is, *"Open!"* To which the teacher again calls, *"Eyeballs!"* And the expected reply from the children is, *"Click!"* With these two words of declaration, the teacher is wooing dull-of-hearing ears and distracted eyes to meander no longer. With their unison response, the students acknowledge that their attention and vision have been diverted to lesser, trivial pursuits as they resolve to refocus their focus.

Sitting still and attentively listening in a Sunday school classroom may feel like an eternity at times to a fidgety seven-year-old, but we would all agree that it is definitely not. Resolving to be focused over the span of forty-five or sixty *minutes* in the class room is admirable, but how does one stay focused on God's call for their life over the span of forty-five or sixty *years?*

PHOROPTERS AND THE WORD OF GOD

Phoropter. Just glancing at the word and sounding it out may conjure up some diverse imagery in our mind's eye. Is it a lesser-known, distant cousin twice-removed of the Velociraptor? Is it one of the umpteen stainless dental instruments that your dentist asks his assistant for once you have plopped down in the chair sporting a stylish clip-on bib? Nope, neither.

A phoropter is an instrument that most of us at one time or another have placed our foreheads against and looked through while sitting in the seat at the eye doctor's office. However precise we imagined our vision to be when we entered the place, the true health and condition of our eyesight is brought to light via this instrument. We may have fancied ourselves to have 20/20 vision or even better, but the phoropter is unbiased and is not influenced by our confident swagger as we smugly plop ourselves down in the vinyl-wrapped chair. When used by an optometrist, there is no guesswork needed as to the condition of our eyesight. Over the course of the next few minutes, the status of our vision will be made unmistakably clear.

God has His spiritual phoropter as well. However, you don't have to use spell checker to write it or hunt down a dictionary for the correct pronunciation. God's phoropter is called the Bible and it is the primary means for Christians to stay focused as we make our way through this sin-marred world.

> *For the word of God is quick, and powerful, and sharper than any twoedged sword, piercing even to the dividing asunder of soul and spirit, and of the joints and marrow, and is a discerner of the thoughts and intents of the heart. Neither is there any creature that is not manifest in his sight: but all things are naked and opened unto the eyes of him with whom we have to do.*—HEBREWS 4:12–13

The Apostle James provides another layer of perspective with these words:

> *But be ye doers of the word, and not hearers only, deceiving your own selves. For if any be a hearer of the word, and not a doer, he is like unto a man beholding his natural face in a glass: For he beholdeth himself, and goeth his way, and straightway forgetteth what manner of man he was. But whoso looketh into the perfect law of liberty, and continueth therein, he being not a forgetful hearer, but a doer of the work, this man shall be blessed in his deed.*—JAMES 1:22–25

While optometrists generally advise us to schedule times behind the phoropter annually, the Great Physician would have the Christian to place himself under His phoropter daily. Psalm 88:9 instructs, *"Mine eye mourneth by reason of affliction: Lord, I have called daily upon thee."* The Bereans were commended for their time each day in the Word of God: *"These were more noble than those in Thessalonica, in that they received the word with all readiness of mind, and searched the scriptures daily, whether those things were so"* (Acts 17:11).

As an optometrist is mindful that our physical eyesight is ever failing, God knows that our spiritual eyesight is likewise prone to falter and in continual need of refocus. And so in loving kindness, He made provision for just that by giving us His eternal, unfailing Word. God instructs the lukewarm, self-satisfied church of Laodicea, *"I counsel thee to…anoint thine eyes with eyesalve, that thou mayest see"* (Revelation 3:18). That cleansing, vision-restoring balm that renews our focus and washes away the dirt, grime, and unprofitable distractions from our eyes was, is, and always will be the pure Word of God: *"That he might sanctify and cleanse it with the washing of water by the word"* (Ephesians 5:26). *"Now ye are clean through the word which I have spoken unto you"* (John 15:3).

What a timeless lesson to be learned for the soul fatigued by years of living a distracted life, void of its God-called purpose! What a needful reminder to the Christian going through the vain motions of day-to-day life, distinctly lacking the Christ-honoring focus God desires for each of His children.

WHAT'S YOUR SPIRITUAL PSI?

Not long ago, I decided to purchase a pressure washer to use occasionally around our home. I headed to the local hardware store, where I was not disappointed in the impressive line-up of models on display. The store boasted everything from an ultra-light apparatus wand that attaches to the end of a garden hose all the way to a beastly machine powered by a bone-jarring nineteen horsepower engine, packing a massive 5,000 PSI (pounds per square inch) and capable of unleashing 5 GPM (gallons per minute). I stood in awe as my mind ran rampant. Over the next couple of minutes, several thoughts raced through my mind:

How on earth have I been able to live life up to this point without this puppy in my possession?

How much would it set me back to add a third-car garage onto our house so that we can have a place to park this metal monstrosity, weighing in about as much as a heifer?

In the hands of a novice, would this device meet the criteria set forth by the military to be classified as a WMD (Weapon of Mass Destruction)?

Is purchasing this machine like buying a firearm for hunting, where I have to register and go through a pressure washer safety course and wear an orange vest and cap while using it?

A salesperson walked over and handed me a paper towel to wipe the drool from my mouth that was trickling down my chin and had begun to form a puddle on the floor below.

He began to dote about what this thing would do. I listened in earnest and midway through the spiel, I asked why there were five different colored tips—white, black, green, yellow, and red. He explained the white one was for dispensing soap through the machine and that black was for general use such as washing a car, while green was for jobs like removing grime off a wooden deck or removing old paint from a fence.

I asked what the yellow tip's purpose was.

At first, he vaguely suggested that perhaps it could be used to remove fresh paint from metal—a form of wet sand-blasting. In our subdivision, nearly everyone had 1 x 4 treated lumber fencing around their yard, and he mentioned that the intensity of the pressure would simply split the boards in two.

My eyebrows perked up in a northerly direction, an outward tell-tale sign of the approval that had already taken place in my heart. I was thoroughly impressed. This was love at first sight. Clearly this was the machine that I was being led to purchase for such a time as this. But one question remained.

I asked what action the red tip performed.

The salesman's countenance changed from exuberance to soberness. He hesitated. No legal, consumer-safe uses for the red tip could be readily cited. Perhaps it was an embellishment, or maybe there was an element of truth to his reply. But he essentially said that if I used the red tip while power washing barefoot, that should I happen to aim it at my foot, it would cut my toes clean off.

Whoa, there, Nelly! As accident-prone as I can be, I knew that no machine, even one as beautifully destructive as this one, was worth losing a bodily extremity over. So, I came back down to earth, lowered my expectations while swallowing my pride, and purchased the 2500 PSI model. I am proud to say that I still have all ten toes safely intact. For now.

What made the difference between the white and the red tip? Why was the white tip safe to use on anything, while the red tip could have been housed behind glass with stenciled letters that read, "Use only in case of emergency"? In a word, it is what we have been talking about in this chapter: focus. The white, black, and green tips were colored as such, because the orifice from which the water flowed was much larger. But on the yellow and red tips, the opening was much smaller, greatly constricting the water and dispensing it with much more focused intensity.

And so it is in the Christian's life. Every Christian is connected to and powered by the Holy Spirit of God. (*"But ye have an unction from the Holy One,"* 1 John 2:20a.) The difference is that some *white-tipped* Christians go through the motions of everyday life distracted, lacking in focused direction and purpose, rendered largely powerless to do much that matters for God and counts for eternity. And then there are those ultra-focused, highly intentional, *red-tipped* Christians. Men and women who live their life in view of a call and have the power of God upon them to make a difference in influencing their families and the world around them for the cause of Christ. Of course, between those two extremes reside black-, green-, and yellow-tipped Christians as well, each life demonstrating various levels of spiritual PSI.

What color is your focus?

MODERN DAY LOTUS EATERS

Within the realm of Greek mythology, the Lotus-eaters were a race of people from an island near North Africa dominated by lotus plants. The lotus fruits and flowers were the primary food of the island and a highly addictive narcotic, lulling the people to sleep in peaceful apathy, entirely removed of all care and concern for their surroundings. As a result, they soon became pleasure addicts—unwittingly enslaved to the intoxicating lure of the lotus flower.

In *Odyssey IX*, Odysseus describes how while he and his men headed west to Ithaca, strong adverse northerly winds blew them off their sailing course:

> I was driven thence by foul winds for a space of nine days upon the sea, but on the tenth day we reached the land of the Lotus-eaters, who live on a food that comes from a kind of flower. Here we landed to take in fresh water, and our crews got their mid-day meal on the shore near the ships.
>
> When they had eaten and drunk I sent two of my company to see what manner of men the people of the place might be, and they had a third man under them. They started at once, and went about among the Lotus-Eaters, who did them no hurt, but gave them to eat of the lotus, which was so delicious that those who ate of it left off caring about home, and did not even want to go back and say what had happened to them, but were for staying and munching lotus with the Lotus-eaters without thinking further of their return; nevertheless, though they wept bitterly I forced them back to the ships and made them fast under the benches. Then I told the rest to go on

board at once, lest any of them should taste of the lotus and leave off wanting to get home, so they took their places and smote the grey sea with their oars.[1]

Odysseus and his men were on a noble quest en route to Ithaca. There was a guided purpose, a clear direction, an intentional pursuit. They were a mission-minded band of brothers out on the high seas adventure of their lifetime. But they encountered tremendous adversity in the form of a streak of nine days of unrelenting northerly winds, resulting in being blown completely off course and dropping anchor in a land where they ought not to have been. They pulled up a chair, sat down and kicked their feet up on the ottoman amongst a room chock full of human sloths. The Bible has much to say about the kind of road-trip buddies that we should (and should not) keep.

> *Blessed is the man that walketh not in the counsel of the ungodly, nor standeth in the way of sinners, nor sitteth in the seat of the scornful.*—Psalm 1:1

> *Be not deceived: evil communications corrupt good manners.*—1 Corinthians 15:33

> *But Amnon had a friend...*—2 Samuel 13:3

Aimlessly off course in their direction and hopelessly off task in their thinking, the men lowered something far more precious than their anchor that day—they lowered their guard. Hmmm…ever been there, done that? Your walk with Christ is sweet. Your steps are guided. Your thought life is pure. Your joy is overflowing. Your way is blessed. Then, in an unsuspecting moment, a foul northerly blows into your life. Perhaps you fight against it for a season, perhaps longer. Perhaps not even at all. Whatever the case, the end result is usually the same as your life drifts off course. Way off course. Things turn ugly as they always do when our once-affixed eyes begin to wander and when the wooing of temptation to stray reaches a fever pitch. We cave. Again.

Fortunately, Lotus-eaters solicited by the draw of selfish pleasure are restricted to the corridors of Greek mythology. Unfortunately, their self-pleasing, apathetic ways do not know such mythical boundaries. All of us can fall prey to purposeless journeys and empty living. Do not let your guard down, as Odysseus' men did. A non-fictional devil is burning the candle at both ends to blow Christian men, women, and young people off the God-orchestrated course for their life. He tirelessly attempts to keep their eyes blind and their minds oblivious to the field that God has for them.

The seeds of the addictive lotus plants are nurtured and take root only in the rich soil of Odyssey fiction. But Satan has no such shortage of narcotic seeds, which, without a God-driven focus, will delight to take root in the fertile soil of one's heart—of *your* heart.

Three of the four gospel accounts feature the story that we call the Parable of the Sower. In Jesus' illustration, the Sower plants seeds (symbolic of the Word of God) in four different soil settings (symbolic of the human heart), and each respond differently to the seeds. Satan is the great imitator, and he too seeks to plant his own hellish seed on a variety of human hearts as well. Oh, be careful little eyes what you see. *Let thine eyes be on the field.*

To give anything less than your best is to sacrifice the gift.
—Steve Prefontaine

It is better to wear out than to rust out.—**Richard Cumberland**

You can't build a reputation on what you are going to do.
—Henry Ford

Opportunity knocks at the strangest times. It's not the time that matters but how you answer the door.—**Steve Gray**

Chance is always powerful. Let your hook be always cast; in the pool where you least expect it, there will be a fish.— **Ovid**

CHAPTER TWO

THE FIELD IS SACRED

But the field…shall be holy unto the LORD, as a field devoted…—LEVITICUS 27:21A

Followers of Christ come in all shapes, sizes, colors, and yes, even in all vocational backgrounds. There are Christian lawyers, teachers, plumbers, athletes, bankers, nurses, sales managers, technicians, customer service representatives, and entrepreneurs, to name but a few. And there is nothing wrong with such vocations. In fact, there is everything good and right and even sacred with these and countless other endeavors—*if* those are the vocations God would have for us. But sooner or later, inevitable problems rear their dreaded heads when there is a gap between our chosen field and that field which God has planned for us. It may come as a complete surprise, but the same God who by His spoken word commanded into existence every fabric of the entire universe has placed a personal calling on every believer that is in Christ Jesus.

For I know the thoughts that I think toward you, saith the Lord, *thoughts of peace, and not of evil, to give you an expected end.*—Jeremiah 29:11

According as he hath chosen us in him before the foundation of the world, that we should be holy and without blame before him in love:—Ephesians 1:4

Wise is the Christian that lives in light of this truth and unreservedly seeks God's face for all decisions, small and great. We have assurance from the Bible that God is not elusive and will reveal His appointed direction for our lives to all who seek His will.

SECULAR MEET SACRED

Too often we segregate the secular from the sacred. Many of us view our activities from 12:01 PM on Sunday (or until the final "amen" in the worship service, whichever should come first) to 10:00 AM the following Lord's Day morning as secular. In other words, sacred pursuits are wrongfully confined to worship services at church and perhaps time spent in private devotions at home. There are 168 hours over the course of seven days— is 1 or 2 hours a week the sum total of our pursuit of sacred endeavors? Does God's plan for His children consist of less than 2 percent of our time on this earth to be spent in sacred devotion and service to Him? If so, then secularism trumps— no, it trounces—the sacred, relegating sacredness as largely inconsequential in the landscape of our daily lives.

Secular is a categorical term cleverly devised by man as a catchall for everything not deemed sacred. And in such a flawed context, pretty much everything would be deemed not sacred. Traditional thinking confines the notion of sacred to only a handful of activities that are explicitly religious. So then all of life's other grand experiences, as well as everyday occurrences, must be dubbed as secular. With this viewpoint having such an illegitimate stronghold on Christian thinking, it is no wonder that many bow down to the awesome influence of the god of secularism. Sure, we offer streaky devotion now and then to Jesus Christ and to all things sacred—but our real god, at least the one we prefer to spend the most time with, resides ever so comfortably in the secular.

Take heart. We are not the inaugural generation guilty of saying one thing and doing another. Nope, we come from a long, inglorious line of fence straddlers. Since the beginning of time, scores of folks have been known to talk the talk and yet fail to walk the walk, content to give lip service to God. As someone has well stated, "Your talk talks, and your walk talks, but your walk talks louder than your talk talks." It was so in Elijah's day, and even Jesus had to contend with it during His earthly ministry.

> Ye hypocrites, well did Esaias prophesy of you, saying, This people draweth nigh unto me with their mouth, and honoureth me with their lips; but their heart is far from me. But in vain they do worship me, teaching for doctrines the commandments of men.
> —MATTHEW 15:7–9

True, we are not the first generation of inconsistent Christians bent on living life smack-dab in the middle of the road, but if our hearts would be resolved to simply obey the things of God and worship Him in spirit and in truth, our generation could be the one that breaks the cycle of inconsistency. This could be the time, and we could be the people where the proverbial buck stops.

The argument for things we once thought of as secular being captive to the sacred is a persuasive one, and I am convinced that a convergence of the secular and sacred is God's vantage point on the whole matter as well. While we often erect mental barriers between the two entities, the God who knows everything knows no such thing. Just to level our thinking, sacred could best be defined as holy or devoted; as in, *"but the field…shall be holy unto the LORD, as a field devoted"* (Leviticus 27:21).

In this context, a field is nothing more than cultivated dirt. What on earth is so sacred about dirt? Outside of an impassioned agronomist looking for the next breakthrough in soil sciences, or an inventive six-year-old with his heart set on serving up some of his world famous mud pies, what is so bedazzling about soil? Perhaps to you and me, not much at all, but to the God who created everything (including dirt) for His enduring glory, all is sacred. *"Thou art worthy, O Lord, to receive glory and honour and power: for thou hast created all things, and for thy pleasure they are and were created"* (Revelation 4:11). When you think of it, God has done some pretty amazing things with dirt. *"And the LORD God formed man of the dust of the ground, and breathed into his nostrils the breath of life; and man became a living soul"* (Genesis 2:7). As God breathes new life in and through His children, I am quite certain He is still able to do some amazing things with us today.

As a living soul created by God, whatever your life's calling, it is of a sacred nature and it matters to God. Knowing this, we should give Him our very best in the workplace and everyplace else. Martin Luther once stated, "The maid who sweeps her kitchen is doing the will of God just as much as the clergy who prays—not because she may sing a Christian hymn as she sweeps but because God loves clean floors. The Christian shoemaker does his Christian duty not by putting little crosses on the shoes, but by making good shoes, because God is interested in good craftsmanship."[1]

God has a vested interest in how His children perform daily tasks at work, in the home, at school, and out in the community—even tasks that our culture has labeled as secular. Don't take my word for it—take His as you meditate on the following verses:

Whatsoever thy hand findeth to do, do it with thy might; for there is no work, nor device, nor knowledge, nor wisdom, in the grave, whither thou goest. —ECCLESIASTES 9:10

Whether therefore ye eat, or drink, or whatsoever ye do, do all to the glory of God. —1 CORINTHIANS 10:31

And whatsoever ye do, do it heartily, as to the Lord, and not unto men; Knowing that of the Lord ye shall receive the reward of the inheritance: for ye serve the Lord Christ. —COLOSSIANS 3:23–24

HOLY GROUND AND
SHOES THAT WALK ON IT

Harry Ironside, one of the great preachers from yesteryear, grew
up in a home with his widowed mother, his father having died
of typhoid when Harry was two years old. When he was not in
school, Harry could be found at the shoemaker shop working
for a cobbler in order to help his mother make ends meet.

Harry's employer, Dan Mackay, was a beam of Christian
light to his community. He was a man who found Christ's
call on his life and was living it for the glory of God. In some
respects, Mackay's tiny little shop could have passed for an
aspiring chapel of sorts, with Scripture posted all along its
humble walls. On the shop's front counter a stack of gospel
tracts nestled beside an open Bible. Every package couriered
from that shop contained a note of Scripture, and rarely did
patrons leave the storefront without hearing the gospel story.

Young Harry's chief duty was to hammer the leather used
for the sole of the shoe. The proper way for making long lasting
soles seems antiquated today, but the process was simple. A
piece of leather was cut to fit the shoe, and then the leather
was placed in a bucket of water to soak. Harry's job was to take
the soaked leather and pound it until it was completely dry, at
which point it was ready to be nailed to the shoe. As you can
imagine, this process of hammering each sole took a long time
and much effort on the part of the young lad, but Mr. Mackay
assured Harry that it was necessary.

Mackay was not the only cobbler in town, but he was
perhaps the only honest one. Another shoe shop faced the road
that Harry walked to and from work. Sometimes Harry would

stop briefly outside the window of the storefront and with unfeigned curiosity glance at the work that was taking place inside. The cobbler who owned this shop seemed to be the antithesis of Mackay—a godless, vile man—and Harry sensed that his shop was run quite differently. Harry noticed that the man never struck the leather soles with so much as one blow from the hammer, but nailed them onto the shoe while they were still soaking wet.

Eureka! Harry discovered a bypass to the nasty case of "cobbler's elbow" he was developing from all the unending (and apparently needless) blows to the leather with the hammer. Harry related the rest of the story in his own words:

> One day I ventured inside, something I had been warned never to do. Timidly, I said, "I notice you put the soles on while still wet. Are they just as good as if they were pounded?" He gave me a wicked leer as he answered, "They come back all the quicker this way, my boy." Feeling I had learned something, I related the instance to my boss and suggested that I was perhaps wasting time in drying out the leather so carefully. Mr. Mackay stopped his work and opened his Bible to the passage, Whatsoever ye do, do all to the glory of God. "Harry," he said, "I do not cobble shoes just for the four bits and six bits [about fifty to seventy-five cents] that I get from my customers. I am doing this for the glory of God. I expect to see every shoe I have ever repaired in a big pile at the judgment seat of Christ, and I do not want the Lord to say to me in that day, "Dan, this was a poor job. You did not do your best here." I want Him to be able to say, "Well done, good and faithful servant." Then he went on to explain that just as some men are called to preach, so he was called to fix shoes, and

that only as he did this well would his testimony count for God.[2]

Bob Jones, Sr., astutely said, "Life is not divided into the secular and sacred. All ground is holy ground, and every bush is a burning bush." Remember the burning bush conversation that took place between God and Moses? *"And he said, Draw not nigh hither: put off thy shoes from off thy feet, for the place whereon thou standest is holy ground"* (Exodus 3:5). Holy ground? You have got to be kidding. Moses was on the backside of the desert! Ground which is sacred? And yet to a Holy, very much non-secular God, everything is to be held sacred. All pursuits matter, and God cares how we carry them out. The Apostle Paul gave a decisive thumbs-down to a 2D perspective on living, which wrongly divides the secular from the sacred: *"And whatsoever ye do in word or deed, do all in the name of the Lord Jesus, giving thanks to God and the Father by him"* (Colossians 3:17).

LIFE IN 3D

What if we were to turn such prevalent and unbiblical thinking upside down? Instead of viewing life as subdivided into all things secular and sacred in 2D, what if we looked upon all the events of daily life in more of a conglomerated fashion in 3D? This convergence of the sacred and secular is foundational and biblical. When we take down the self-fabricated construction cones in our mind dividing the sacred and the secular, we release the stranglehold that the secular has held for far too long on the sacred. And in so doing, we permit the sacred the free reign God intended, allowing it to permeate each and every remarkable, as well as routine, aspect of our lives, shifting our perspective around why we do what we do.

Is there anything sacred about a born-again child of God who underwrites insurance, operates a bulldozer, raises cattle, writes human resource policies, drives a cab, prepares tax returns, fills in potholes, drafts engineering specs, manages sales, or does HVAC repair? Yes! Yes! And again, yes! If that is God's calling and they wake up each day dead-set on doing such for His glory. All these fields and more are holy, and they are sacred indeed. I like A.W. Tozer's comment on this: "We must do worldly jobs, but if we do them with sanctified minds, they become offerings to God."

When we put on our 3D glasses and look at things from God's perspective, we'll no longer subdivide our lives in such a way that keeps God in the nosebleed section for ninety-eight percent of our weekly existence. As we continue to view each moment and every aspect of daily living as sacred, we'll see God make His way from the nosebleed seats in Section 317/Row YY of our lives, down to the Owner's box where He rightfully belongs.

Right now, at this very moment, you are as close to God as you want to be. James 4:8 promises, *"Draw nigh to God, and he will draw nigh to you."* When we take a little step of faith toward God, He moves a giant leap toward us, because His stride is a whole lot bigger than ours. And adopting the viewpoint that everything in this life is sacred to God—and to us—is no small step of faith. Friend, you have a field. And in God's eyes, that field has long since been considered sacred. Isn't it about time it was so in your eyes?

Destiny is no matter of chance. It is a matter of choice. It is not a thing to be waited for; it is a thing to be achieved.
—William Jennings Bryan

When written in Chinese, the word "crisis" is composed of two characters. One represents danger and the other represents opportunity.—**John Fitzgerald Kennedy**

Far better is it to dare mighty things, to win glorious triumphs, even though checkered by failure…than to rank with those poor spirits who neither enjoy much nor suffer much, because they live in a gray twilight that knows not victory nor defeat.
—Theodore Roosevelt

CHAPTER THREE

CONSIDER THE FIELD

*She considereth a field, and buyeth it: with the fruit of
her hands she planteth a vineyard.*—PROVERBS 31:16

You've been there. There you stand in the supermarket
check-out line. As you patiently wait your turn, nearby
tabloids with their shock and awe headlines catch your eye.
Lose twenty-five pounds by the weekend. Another celebrity
marriage. Another celebrity break-up. UFOs surround the
skies of downtown Los Angeles with alien abductions reported.
(This one just might have some credence.)

Your eyes shift to the rows of strategically placed snacks.
A candy bar wasn't on your shopping list; neither were the
breath mints or fingernail clippers. Yet, on impulse, into the
basket they go.

Retail marketers have appropriately dubbed this
transaction an impulse buy. Your purchase of these last-minute
items was not planned or pre-meditated. Rather, it took place

on impulse with little or no consideration. Impulse buys for a stick of beef jerky, a bottle of pain reliever, or spearmint chewing gum are generally not decisions which require significant deliberation. A last minute decision to pick up lip balm and batteries is not apt to haunt you with regret the rest of your days (or even the rest of that day). You won't lose sleep tonight because you didn't fast and pray over these decisions.

But it seems that in too many instances we do not invest nearly enough careful, deliberate, soul-searching reflection when it comes to matters of greater consequence—matters such as finding a field or vocational calling for your life.

STEP BY STEP

Proverbs 31 introduces us to a godly woman of great character. She is faithful to her husband, committed to her role as a mother, believing both to be of the utmost importance and one of her highest callings. She is generous toward others and tireless in her efforts to bless and nurture her family. Kindness and wisdom flow in the wake of her every move. Each aspect of her integrity, described over a full twenty-two verses, indicates that she is a woman who lives life intentionally and with due consideration. Everything about her affirms that she is a purposeful, deliberate lady who is not content to go about her day, much less her life, simply winging it.

Verse 16 tells us that before she buys a field, she carefully considers it. Unlike many of her contemporaries, she is not given to impulse buying. We don't know if this is the first parcel of land she has bought, but it appears it is not the first field she has considered. Her deliberation suggests that her buying decision was some time in the making. Her real estate agent must have been utterly fatigued and at her wits' end, having all but run out of every last available MLS listing to show her.

Time and again in Scripture, God's Spirit impresses upon individuals to consider, meditate, look upon, and invest of themselves in their fields.

> *Let thine eyes be on the field…*—RUTH 2:9

> *…Lift up your eyes, and look on the fields…* —JOHN 4:35

> *…Come, and let us go out into the field…* —1 SAMUEL 20:11

> *Come, my beloved, let us go forth into the field…* —SONG OF SOLOMON 7:11

It's true that the context in each of the above verses is that of a physical field—an actual parcel of land. But God often seeks to kindle our mindfulness that He has a vocational field for us—a work to immerse ourselves in for His enduring glory.

The call from on high begins with our careful consideration of His field for us. This first step leads to an amazing journey that God has in store. And while it is true that it is only the first of many steps, it is a significant one—a milestone event.

Consider the excitement of proud parents when their toddler takes his or her first steps. They capture a video or photo and quickly post to social media sites. They call family members and close friends to let them know the big news. And everyone's heart is thrilled.

Is it a stretch to envision that when God's children cross a milestone life event, our Heavenly Father is also excited at His children taking their first steps and making forward progress in the faith? Unlike human parents, our Heavenly Father in His foreknowledge knew exactly when this day would come. Nonetheless, it still brings joy to the heart of God to see His children stepping out in faith and taking early strides in obedience to His truth. *"I have no greater joy than to hear that my children walk in truth"* (3 John 1:4).

Too many of us never actually cross that milestone in our thinking. Somewhere following high school or perhaps after college, we settle into a job, get married, have a child (or two) get a mortgage (or two), and find ourselves on a career path from which we simply cannot spot any marked exits. And even if we did see a sign indicating an exit ahead, it can feel as though life has us stuck bumper to bumper across six lanes of rush hour traffic.

Or, worse than being sandwiched in traffic, is that we find ourselves going the wrong way on a one-way street against the flow of traffic. Like the young man who was walking along a country road, and as he did, a farmer driving a wagon passed by. Without asking permission, the young man jumped on the wagon and said, "I'm going to ride with you to Louisville." The farmer just looked at him and said nothing. They rode on for ten miles. The young man began to feel uneasy. He turned to the farmer and said, "I say old pop, how much farther is it to Louisville?" The farmer replied, "If you keep in the direction you are going, it is about 25,000 miles; but if you get off and walk back the other way, it is only about sixteen miles—six miles from where you jumped on."[1]

I know that life is a highway, but sometimes we just jump on for a ride without first finding out where it is going to take us. God has a good destination mapped out for us already, and the onus is on us to make sure we follow His leading.

CAR WASHES AND ARCHERY RANGES: FINDING DIRECTION IN THE MOST UNLIKELY OF PLACES

For six wonderful years, I called the rapidly growing town of Cypress, Texas—a suburb in the upper northwest side of Houston—home. An automated car wash had been newly built less than a mile from the house, and I would frequent the wash, as I never had to leave the comfort of my driver's seat.

After dropping in the token and pulling forward, there was that heavy-pressure spray coming from below to clean the underneath of my vehicle. As the spray did its work, I continued pulling forward about twenty feet until the next step of the car wash initiated. Because of the heavy spray, it could be hard to see where you were going. This was especially true in the winter as the warm mist from below combined with the cool air above to form dense condensation. For this reason, the owner installed an electronic sign at the back of the bay displaying three arrows. If I drifted too far to the right, a left arrow flashed, indicating for me to turn in that direction. Ditto if I drifted too far to the right. If I was dead on course, then there was an arrow signaling straight ahead, indicating to keep in the direction I was going.

Even with the blinking arrows, the under-spray could be so heavy that it was difficult to know which direction to steer. It was essential to maintain a steady, fixed focus on the arrows, for without them, the short distance I had to go could find me getting off track, running into the tire guard rails, or moving forward with uncertainty. Fortunately, in all the times that I washed my car there, the arrows proved to be a trusted, reliable source to guide me.

Like the condensation in the car wash, the pressures and uncertainties of life can cause us to become disoriented and not really know what step to take next, where to turn, or which direction to go. It's not by coincidence that verses such as these have been divinely placed in the Bible for our benefit: *"Let thine eyes look right on, and let thine eyelids look straight before thee. Ponder the path of thy feet, and let all thy ways be established. Turn not to the right hand nor to the left"* (Proverbs 4:25–27). God has a wonderfully designated path for us and desires to lovingly guide us along the unfamiliar way.

And I will bring the blind by a way that they knew not;
I will lead them in paths that they have not known:

I will make darkness light before them, and crooked things straight. These things will I do unto them, and not forsake them.—ISAIAH 42:16

The Lord would have His children stay close by His side so that we can hear the Holy Spirit whisper to us. *"And thine ears shall hear a word behind thee, saying, This is the way, walk ye in it"* (Isaiah 30:21).

In an attempt to keep us from listening to God's direction, the enemy of our souls is constantly shooting under spray at us to disorient us and get us off track. The devil's under-spray can assume many manifestations including selfishness, temptations, distractions, diversions, vanity, discouragement, and fear. Numerous unwitting Christians proceed recklessly through these challenges of life. We do not earnestly consider God's directional arrows and are not sensitive to His guardrails placed for our protection and to guide us in the way that we should go.

Scripture sounds a warning to people who seek Him at only a superficial level. These are the folks who want just enough of Jesus to help them be successful or to overcome some obstacle, sickness, or other difficulties they are confronting at the present moment. But they do not want Him to really interfere with the course of their lives. It is a tragic blunder to seek God's direction half-heartedly or in an agenda-driven, self-serving manner. *"But if from thence thou shalt seek the LORD thy God, thou shalt find him, if thou seek him with all thy heart and with all thy soul"* (Deuteronomy 4:29).

If you have a heart-level resolve to do what God would have you to do, then you are apt to come across the FSBO (For Sale by Owner) sign in God's chosen field for you.

Let's look at yet another account of Scripture and learn how to look for His arrows. Young David was trying to determine the next right step in his life. He had been employed by his best friend Jonathan's father, King Saul, but it was something of an on again-off again kind of relationship.

When King Saul grew weary of issuing David a W-2 form, on more than one occasion, he launched a javelin at him. After playing a couple rounds of dodge-javelin, David did not know what to do or which direction to turn. Did God want him to continue to stick-it out, knowing he might literally get *stuck* if he did; or was God trying to move him on? We pick up the account in 1 Samuel 20, as Jonathan speaks these words to his best friend, David.

> *And I will shoot three arrows on the side thereof, as though I shot at a mark. And, behold, I will send a lad, saying, Go, find out the arrows. If I expressly say unto the lad, Behold, the arrows are on this side of thee, take them; then come thou: for there is peace to thee, and no hurt; as the LORD liveth. But if I say thus unto the young man, Behold, the arrows are beyond thee; go thy way: for the LORD hath sent thee away….. And it came to pass in the morning, that Jonathan went out into the field at the time appointed with David, and a little lad with him. And he said unto his lad, Run, find out now the arrows which I shoot. And as the lad*

ran, he shot an arrow beyond him. And when the lad was come to the place of the arrow which Jonathan had shot, Jonathan cried after the lad, and said, Is not the arrow beyond thee? And Jonathan cried after the lad, Make speed, haste, stay not. And Jonathan's lad gathered up the arrows, and came to his master. But the lad knew not any thing: only Jonathan and David knew the matter. —1 SAMUEL 20:20–22, 35–39

Although Jonathan pulled back the bowstring, verse 22 tells us that it was the Lord that superintended the distance of the arrows. Perhaps God has been shooting directional arrows in your life in an effort to point you in the way which He would have you to go. If so, you must be discerning and look past the under-spray the enemy is shooting at you. The challenge from Scripture is to carefully consider the field. "*Wherefore be ye not unwise, but understanding what the will of the Lord is*" (Ephesians 5:17). Stop brushing aside the Holy Spirit's guiding presence. Remove any self-imposed blinders to His leading. Be done with finger pointing or blame shifting. Enough with having your eyes shut to the direction in which God is so plainly leading.

THE STRENGTH OF A THREEFOLD CORD

We see the principle of strength in numbers clearly set forth in Scripture. "*And if one prevail against him, two shall withstand him; and a threefold cord is not quickly broken*" (Ecclesiastes 4:12).

I don't think it is fair or biblically honest to always attempt to formulize Scripture and reduce the victorious Christian life to a paint-by-numbers approach. But there is a principle in this passage that we can apply to seeking God's direction. Let's take a closer look at what we briefly discussed in the previous chapter regarding Jeremiah 29. In it, we will see that this passage contains three strong "cords" for the Christian who desires more than anything to find God's calling.

Cord #1: SERVING God with all of our hearts through work.

> *For I know the thoughts that I think toward you, saith the* Lord, *thoughts of peace, and not of evil, to give you an expected end.*—JEREMIAH 29:11

I'll be honest and upfront. The last two cords we'll look at are predictable. You're clever, and I am confident that you will spot them coming from a mile away. No *Aha* moment awaits you. But work? I'm guessing this cord came out of nowhere in your thinking and took you by surprise. God's *expected end* for each of us is further revealed and comes into more vivid detail when we serve Him right where we are. "*Commit thy works unto the* Lord, *and thy thoughts shall be established*" (Proverbs 16:3). God gives clarity of mind to those who have a mind to work. (See Nehemiah 4:6.)

Nowhere in the Bible do we see God work mightily through the lazy or slothful. God comes alongside, empowers, and equips His people while they are already in motion and working. Gideon was scared and more than a little timid, but God's call on his life was revealed while he was threshing wheat (Judges 6:11–12). Elisha and twelve yoke of oxen were plowing in the field when God directed the prophet Elijah to pass the baton (or pass the mantle) to him (1 Kings 19:19). Saul's calling was made known while he was busy searching for his father's lost donkeys (1 Samuel 9:2). David was shepherding his father's sheep when Samuel came to anoint him king (1 Samuel 16:10). The accounts of other men and women whom God met with and called while they were already busily serving and working are well-nigh inexhaustible. The list of individuals whom God called while they were eating bon-bons and setting personal best records on *Candy Crush Saga* are non-existent.

We will have more to say about the importance of work in chapter 5, but suffice it to say that God is looking for laborers: "*Then saith he unto his disciples, The harvest truly is plenteous, but the labourers are few; Pray ye therefore the Lord of the harvest, that he will send forth labourers into his harvest*" (Matthew 9:37–38). When we roll up our sleeves and serve God with all of our heart where we are at now, He will show us the next step.

Cord #2: SEEKING God with all of our hearts in prayer.

Then shall ye call upon me, and ye shall go and pray unto me, and I will hearken unto you.—JEREMIAH 29:12

Consider this a reminder that the avenue to God and His will for our lives is paved through prayer. No casual kind of praying will do when it comes to getting a hold of God. We must be all-in and whole-hearted.

Cord #3: SPENDING time with God with all of our heart in His Word.

> *And ye shall seek me, and find me, when ye shall search for me with all your heart.*—JEREMIAH 29:13

While prayer is largely me talking to God, reading His Word is God talking to me. "*Thy word is a lamp unto my feet, and a light unto my path*" (Psalms 119:105). "*The entrance of thy words giveth light; it giveth understanding unto the simple*" (Psalms 119:130). But just like prayer, no casual kind of Bible reading will do. Ever read an entire chapter or two (or ten), closed your Bible, and literally not have a clue as to what you just read? Me too. That's because our hearts were not in it, and we were distracted.

UNDER NEW OWNERSHIP

There is a story from long ago where an old Scottish woman went from home to home across the countryside selling thread, buttons, and shoestrings. When she came to an unmarked crossroad, she would toss a stick into the air and go in the direction the stick pointed when it landed. One day, however, she was seen tossing the stick up several times. "*Why do you toss the stick more than once?*" someone asked. "Because," replied the woman, "It keeps pointing to the left, and I want to take the road on the right." She dutifully kept throwing the stick into the air until it pointed the way she wanted to go.

The time for our self-will exerting itself in our lives is gone. *"The night is far spent, the day is at hand: let us therefore cast off the works of darkness, and let us put on the armour of light"* (Romans 13:12). It is time to go where God wants you to go. It is time to be what He wants you to be. It is time to do what He wants you to do. The Lord Jesus Christ did not endure the cruel death of the cross so that you and I could live any old way of our own choosing. He gave His life so that we might live afresh and new for Him. *"Therefore if any man be in Christ, he is a new creature: old things are passed away; behold, all things are become new"* (2 Corinthians 5:17). He suffered and bled and died so that we might have newness of life and live in light of this truth.

I have been privileged to call several different states home, including Indiana, Texas, Michigan, Ohio, Missouri, and Louisiana. Every time we have moved, my wife and I believed we were following the Lord's leading the best we knew how, and yet every move was difficult. It was tough to bid farewell to dear friends and church families that we had come to know and love. It was also difficult to say goodbye to familiar surroundings and amenities, especially our home with the memories we made there and the labor of love, prayer, and sweat that held it all together.

One home we waved goodbye to stands out. With 3,200 square feet, it had become our dream home and a little bit of heaven on earth. The interior appearance and creature comforts of our home were rivaled only by the exceptional curb appeal of the stately exterior. A beautifully designed mosaic of brick and stonework enveloped the large two-story structure with surrounding pine trees that stretched high up into the south Texas sky and a lawn with not so much as a trace of even a solitary rogue weed.

And then amidst the most beautiful of residential settings, some real estate agent went and drove deep into the soil of our lawn (and even deeper into our hearts) a repulsive looking *For Sale* sign. Dream over.

After nearly twenty years in the corporate world, the Lord had called me into full time ministry to preach the gospel. With that call, some of the comforts we had enjoyed would now be out of reach as a pastor supporting a family of six. I never will forget closing day and signing over the ownership papers. At the title company's office, my wife and I sat across the table from the buyer as we had done many times before, but this was different. What was at stake here was no ordinary signing. A line had been drawn in the sand concerning the direction of our lives, and knowing this, we were willingly crossing over. A thick air of finality lingered in the room that day, as my wife and I signed everything over to the new owner.

In the weeks to come, I would hear from my old neighbors concerning changes that the new owner was making. He did what? He cut down that gorgeous tall pine tree in the front yard? He ripped out all the new carpet on the first floor and put in wood flooring? Are you serious? He tore up the lush, weed-free Bermuda grass in the back yard and put in a huge swimming pool? (Okay, I actually have to give the thumbs-up to that improvement. But all the other remodeling changes, not so much.) Who does he think he is, anyway? Oh yeah. Almost forgot. He's the new owner.

In the wake of this life-altering decision and subsequent chain of events, I was reminded of some simple truths. While I owned the home, it was mine to do with as I pleased because as owner, I was the boss. But then I decided to sell it. On closing day when the new owner took possession, I turned over the deed, the schematics to the underground sprinkler system, and the key to the front door to him. The home is now his. He can make any changes he desires. He can do with it as he pleases. Perhaps I approve of what he is doing and his plans for the future, or maybe not; either way I have no viable say in the matter because the home is no longer mine. It's now his.

That's the way it must be with your life and mine. The truth behind 2 Corinthians 5:17 is that when we give our life to Christ, in effect, we turn over the title deed, the schematics to all our days ahead, and the keys of our life to Jesus—the new Owner. Anyone who ever genuinely came to Christ in the pages of Scripture experienced such a life change. There were old things that were out and new things that were brought in. It is simply part and parcel of giving up ownership to that of another.

Instead of trying to hang onto the key and the ensuing saga and ongoing power struggle with our new Landlord, our time would be far better spent crying out to God as did Paul,

"And I said, What shall I do, Lord? And the Lord said unto me, Arise, and go into Damascus; and there it shall be told thee of all things which are appointed for thee to do" (Acts 22:10). The problem is, few Christians are willing to go to where God wants us to go because we are dead-set on going the direction of our choosing…like maybe Tarshish.

LIFE IN TARSHISH

Most everyone knows the account of Jonah and the whale. Jonah is a book consisting of just four short chapters, and yet, the story is unforgettable, and the lessons from Jonah innumerable.

Jonah was the original, *I'll do what I want to do and go where I want to go,* genre of rebel. God's directional arrows were unmistakably clear as He instructed Jonah to go to the city of Ninevah, and Jonah, well, Jonah went as far as anyone could go in the opposite direction.

> *Now the word of the LORD came unto Jonah the son of Amittai, saying, Arise, go to Nineveh, that great city, and cry against it; for their wickedness is come up before me. But Jonah rose up to flee unto Tarshish from the presence of the LORD, and went down to Joppa; and he found a ship going to Tarshish: so he paid the fare thereof, and went down into it, to go with them unto Tarshish from the presence of the LORD.*
> —JONAH 1:1–3

Bible commentators largely agree to disagree on the exact location of Tarshish. But some suggest Tarshish was the area of land which today we know as the British Isles. If such is the case, Tarshish was not only the opposite direction of Ninevah, it was as far as one could go from that city in the then known world. Look at the progression, or more aptly the digression, of Jonah's decision making: *"But Jonah rose up to flee unto Tarshish from the presence of the LORD, and went down to Joppa; and he found a ship going to Tarshish: so he paid the fare thereof, and went down into it, to go with them unto Tarshish from the presence of the LORD"* (Jonah 1:3).

He arose and fled—In completely the opposite direction that God was shooting His arrows.

He went down—*Down* is the direction our running from God will always take us.

He found a ship—Jonah looked for a way out and found it. Satan is ever so quick to come alongside and *help* us find a way out of God's will for our lives.

He paid the fare—There was a cost involved in his disobedience, and he showed no signs of suffering from buyer's remorse.

He went—He sealed his fate. He could have easily turned back at any time, and God would have not chastised him. Jonah was a living testimony to the fact that sin will take you farther than you ever intended to go, keep you longer than you ever wanted to stay, and cost you more than you ever imagined to pay.

But then, the grace of God confronted Jonah in a great storm (Jonah 1:4–16) and ultimately in the most unlikely of physical manifestations, a great fish (Jonah 1:17). Recognizing these events as the undeniable hand of God, Jonah never did quite make it to Tarshish. It is clear in the second chapter that Jonah came to a fork in the road in his own life, and at last he surrendered. He finally came to the realization that running from God is always a losing race. We can spend our entire life running, yet wherever our worn out running shoes take us, God is still there.

> *Whither shall I go from thy spirit? or whither shall I flee from thy presence? If I ascend up into heaven, thou art there: if I make my bed in hell, behold, thou art there. If I take the wings of the morning, and dwell in the uttermost parts of the sea; Even there shall thy hand lead me, and thy right hand shall hold me.*—PSALM 139:7–10

Which direction is your life headed right now? Tarshish, representing life done your way? Or Ninevah, symbolizing life lived God's way? Someone once wisely put it, "Even more important than where you stand, is which direction it is that you are going." Many Christians are racking up frequent flyer miles with their many trips en route to Tarshish.

I appreciate true, time-tested expressions like, "Where God guides, He provides," "God's will done God's way will never lack God's supply" and "God pays for what He orders." But remember that God never sent Jonah to Tarshish, and neither is He giving you the nod to head that wayward direction either. Like Jonah then, the fare to Tarshish today is steep, and we are on our own when picking up the tab for that one. The greatest cost for us while living in the land of Tarshish is not so much the financial as it is the time wasted, the opportunities lost, and relational distancing from God while we are living the life of a fugitive on the run.

As a Christian travelling through life the wrong way on a one-way street, one of your most gripping fears should be to celebrate your sixtieth, seventieth, or even eightieth birthday and find that you are still running the opposite direction from the dream that God gave you. Diane Ackerman once said, "I don't want to get to the end of my life and find that I have just lived the length of it. I want to have lived the width of it as well." There are individuals whose lives seem to have been cut tragically short, but most folks live life the full *length* of it. How exceptionally rare and precious it is to witness a Christian man or woman experience the full *width* of God's plan for their lives as well.

HUMAN HISTORY IN A NUTSHELL

The entire history of world events could be boiled down to this description—the Spirit of God moving in fulfillment of God's plan for His creation while Satan moves in opposition to that plan. If such is true for all of God's creation, how much more for His chief creation, mankind.

The first half of the description above declares that God has a perfect plan in mind for you that has been in play since eternity past: *"For we are his workmanship, created in Christ Jesus unto good works, which God hath before ordained that we should walk in them"* (Ephesians 2:10).

The second half of the same statement adds the sobering reality that Satan is relentless with his intent to thwart God's perfect plan for your life. He wants you to comfortably settle into the densely populated metroplex of mediocrity. Thus, the warning, *"Be sober, be vigilant; because your adversary the devil, as a roaring lion, walketh about, seeking whom he may devour"* (1 Peter 5:8). Satan's ongoing work of sidetracking and sabotage is displayed in the gospel of Mark: *"The sower soweth the word. And these are they by the way side, where the word is sown; but when they have heard, Satan cometh immediately, and taketh away the word that was sown in their hearts* (Mark 4:14–15)." Don't be mistaken. Satan isn't content with only snatching away the seed of the gospel that has been sown in a sinner's heart; he also wages war against Christians' hearts attempting to hush the voice of God speaking to His children through the indwelling presence of the Holy Spirit. On either battle front, Satan not only strives to silence God's voice, he schemes to replace God's commanding voice with his own corrupt voice, the voice of the world.

TRAVELING THROUGH VANITY FAIR

In John Bunyan's classic allegory, *The Pilgrim's Progress*, pleasurable trappings hold their victims captive in the town of Vanity. In that futile town a daily festival is held that is known as Vanity-Fair. The main character, Christian, travels through this place of amusement entirely given over to vanity and takes it all in. Bunyan describes the scene for us.

> ...a fair wherein should be sold of all sorts of vanity, and that it should last all the year long. Therefore at this fair are all such merchandise sold as houses, lands, trades, places, honours, preferments, titles, countries, kingdoms; lusts, pleasures, and delights of all sorts, such as, whores, bawds, wives, husbands, children, masters, servants, lives, blood, bodies, souls, silver, gold, pearls, precious stones, and what not. And moreover at this fair, there is at all times to be seen juggling, cheats, games, plays, fools, apes, knaves, and rogues, and that of every kind... This fair, therefore, is an ancient thing, of long standing, and a very great fair.[2]

Whether travelling through the allegorical city known as Vanity or making our way through the everyday encounters and trappings of life in the twenty-first century, the warning signs are clearly posted for all who care to read and heed.

> *Love not the world, neither the things that are in the world. If any man love the world, the love of the Father is not in him. For all that is in the world, the lust of the flesh, and the lust of the eyes, and the pride of life, is not of the Father, but is of the world.*
> —1 JOHN 2:15–16

HOW'S YOUR AIM?

In 2004 at the Olympics hosted in Athens, Greece, American Rifle Shooter, Matt Emmons, had the gold medal in his sights. He was one shot from claiming victory in the 50-meter three-position rifle event. He didn't even need a bull's-eye to win. To take home the gold, his final shot merely needed to strike somewhere on the target. For an Olympian level athlete, this was a gimme. This was a sure thing, if ever there was one in Olympic competition. The coveted gold medal was well within reach, as the Olympic band blew saliva out of their brass instruments while warming up to play "The Star Spangled Banner" in recognition of pending USA gold. No doubt much of his life, at least for the past several years, had been spent in painstaking efforts to reach this point in this competition.

Matt's finger tightened on the trigger. He took careful aim and fired. Under normal circumstances, the shot probably would have received a score of 8.1, much more than enough for a gold medal. But these circumstances were anything but normal. In what was described as, "an extremely rare mistake in elite competition," with the entire world watching on, Emmons' bullet hit target—unfortunately the wrong target. Emmons stood in lane two and squarely hit the target that just so happened to reside in lane three. His aim was dead on. His accuracy was textbook. His target…not so much.

The score given to hitting the bull's eye of a wrong target in Olympic competition is Zero. Nada. Zilch. Null. Zip. Instead of Emmons standing on top of the podium and through tears, seeing the proud display of the beloved stars and stripes amidst chants of USA, it was the Chinese national anthem that rang out that fateful day. Emmons took the whole scene in from the bleachers, not the podium, as he ended up in medal-less eighth place.

Heartbreaking? Yep. Sobering? Understatement of the year. Worst sucker punch ever? It has my vote. But what was the rarest of Olympiad anomalies for one individual is a common occurrence in the lives of countless followers of the Lord Jesus Christ. Every day in newspapers across the country, obituaries are printed of men and women whose lives could be accurately summed up with the sobering headline: *Her aim was spotless, her shot was faultless, and her target was thoughtless.* Christians everywhere are aiming at the wrong life's target and hitting the bull's-eye. Dr. Charles Keene of Bearing Precious Seed Ministries put it like this, "I am not afraid of being a failure. I am afraid at being a success at something God is not interested in."

There are numerous *successful* Christians who, over the course of their lives, garner the attention and wonderment of those around them. But the issue is this: were they successful in things that God cares about? Did they light up the bull's-eye of the right target? Did they live out each and every day to its God-commissioned fullest, faithfully working in their field to achieve the calling of God upon their life? Take it from Matt Emmons—world class accuracy is of no earthly (or heavenly) value if the target in your sights is wrong. Consider your field.

Opportunity comes like a snail, and once it has passed you, it changes into a fleet rabbit and is gone.—**Arthur Brisbane**

You are younger today than you ever will be again. Make use of it.—**Anonymous**

If you can find a path with no obstacles, it probably doesn't lead anywhere.—**Frank A. Clark**

We are continually faced by great opportunities brilliantly disguised as insoluble problems.—**Anonymous**

The greatest mistake you can make in life is to be continually fearing you will make one.—**Elbert Hubbard**

CHAPTER FOUR

BUY THE FIELD

*She considereth a field, and buyeth it: with the fruit of
her hands she planteth a vineyard.*—PROVERBS 31:16

O nce you have considered a field carefully and see that
your treasure and heart have been buried there—*buy
it*. BUY THE FIELD! Stop with the waffling, contingency
planning, second-guessing, and the endless *what-if* scenarios
and buy the field. "*How long halt ye between two opinions?*"
(1 Kings 18:21). Stop kicking the tires already, and step out in
faith and do what God would have you to do.

WILL POWER

A man who was never found tarrying between two opinions
was William Borden. In 1904 when Borden graduated from a
Chicago area high school, his parents gave him a trip around

the world as a graduation present. As Borden traveled through Asia, the Middle East, and Europe, he felt a growing burden for those who had never heard the saving gospel of Jesus Christ. Obedient to his call, young Will drafted a letter home about his desire to become a missionary. Friends responded to this note with expressed disbelief that Will would throw his life away as a missionary. Reflecting on his decision and the reception of others towards it, Borden wrote two simple words in the back of his Bible: "No Reserves."

During Borden's years at Yale, he continued to grow in the things of the Lord. One day he wrote in his journal: "Say 'no' to self and 'yes' to Jesus every time." He did exactly that. Borden witnessed for the Lord Jesus Christ on campus and inspired others to make their lives count for God. One of his classmates said of him: "He certainly was one of the strongest characters I have ever known, and he put backbone into the rest of us at college. There was real iron in him, and I always felt he was of the stuff martyrs were made of, and heroic missionaries of more modern times." Someone who follows the call of God for their life and takes a stand still attracts followers today and inspires others to greater things.

Borden's missionary call became refined and settled as he sensed God's leading to the Muslim Kansu people in China. Upon graduation from Yale, Borden was true to his call to missions and turned down some high-paying job opportunities. In his Bible, next to his previous entry of "No reserves," he wrote two more words: "No retreats."

William Borden went on to do graduate work at Princeton Seminary in New Jersey. When he had finished his studies at Princeton, he set sail for China. It was on his heart to work with unreached Muslims. While stopped in Egypt to study Arabic, Will was fell deathly ill and was diagnosed with spinal meningitis. Within a month, William Borden died at the age of twenty-five; however, the testimony of his life story did not. When the news of Borden's death was cabled back to the u.s., nearly every major American newspaper wrote of the story. "A wave of sorrow went round the world. Borden not only gave [away] his wealth, but himself, in a way so joyous and natural that it [seemed] a privilege rather than a sacrifice," wrote Mary Taylor in her introduction to his biography.

Prior to his death, Borden wrote two more words in his Bible. Underneath "No reserves" and "No retreats," he had penned one final thought. These two compelling words have served to inspire young men and women to yield their lives to the movement of missions. Two simple, dying words: "No regrets."

The individual who accepts the challenge of Scripture and willingly offers all earthly means back unto the Lord— one who keeps no reserves—is a rare and precious soul indeed.

Lay not up for yourselves treasures upon earth, where moth and rust doth corrupt, and where thieves break through and steal: But lay up for yourselves treasures in heaven, where neither moth nor rust doth corrupt, and where thieves do not break through nor steal: For

where your treasure is, there will your heart be also.
—MATTHEW 6:19–21

The follower of Jesus who not only is without any reserves, but also leaves no allowance for going back on his decision—no retreats—is truly a rare genre of Christian. *"And Jesus said unto him, No man, having put his hand to the plough, and looking back, is fit for the kingdom of God"* (Luke 9:62).

A Christian who makes and keeps these two decisions—giving away all reserves and making no retreats—will, at the end of life, also have no regrets. Simply put, there are no regrets for living a life of complete surrender. And this kind of Christian, well, that is amongst the rarest of all jewels within the entirety of Christendom.

After crippling financial losses in the early 1990s, and a leveraged buyout in 1995, Borden, Inc. divested itself of its various divisions and business entities. Considered the world's largest dairy and pasta producer at one time, Borden Inc. exited the corporate scene and is no more. There were no doubt many fine individuals sporting the last name of Borden employed there, but odds are that we would be at a loss to recall the first name of even one of them. But one Borden stood out—young Will, because he followed God's call on his life and bought the field. I believe he was in good company with the likes of the Apostle Paul. From within his lonely Roman prison cell, Paul penned these final, regret-free words:

For I am now ready to be offered, and the time of my departure is at hand. I have fought a good fight, I have

finished my course, I have kept the faith: Henceforth
there is laid up for me a crown of righteousness, which
the Lord, the righteous judge, shall give me at that
day: and not to me only, but unto all them also that
love his appearing.—2 TIMOTHY 4:6–8

Would to God we would have a new generation of believers rise up and live their life with the same galvanizing mantra: *No reserves. No retreats. No regrets.*

MEET AND GREET DEJA VU

Unlike Borden, many believers are completely sidetracked and go through life off target. They have never lifted their eyes and prayerfully considered the vocational field that God ordained for them long before they took their first breath. God told Jeremiah, *"Before I formed thee in the belly I knew thee; and before thou camest forth out of the womb I sanctified thee"* (Jeremiah 1:5). Praise God for those exceptional individuals, such as Borden and others, some unknown to man but famous in the roll call of Heaven, whose lives are a wondrous inspiration to those around them (and to those who would one day follow them). The testimonies of such individuals serve as a catalyst for us to not only consider the field but to pay the price, whatever the cost, by the grace of God, and buy the field.

The considerate woman from Proverbs 31 who we noticed in chapter 3 is such a person of inspiration. Twenty-two verses in this passage of Scripture are given to memorialize her for the godly woman she was. One of the most revealing attributes of her acclaim is found in verse sixteen: "*She considereth a field, and buyeth it: with the fruit of her hands she planteth a vineyard.*"

The challenge from the previous chapter was to give ourselves to much prayerful consideration in search of what God would have us to do with our life. The true rationale for why she has been brought to our attention is the fact that she actually followed through, counted the cost, and *bought* the field. She wouldn't have received a footnote or so much as an honorable mention if Scripture had spoken of her, "She considereth a field, but was one chiefly given to trifling delay and indecision, and alas, never did follow through." Careful, prayerful consideration serves to cultivate the soil of one's heart for a decision. It is a personal choice we each must make concerning the field that has been revealed to us.

Volumes of lamentable commentaries could be written about Christians who came face to face with their God given destiny, tallied the costs, and got sticker shock. They arrived at the conclusion that the asking price of God's will for them was on the steep side. They were not about to pay full MSRP (manufacturer suggested retail price). It's not that they *couldn't* make the purchase, but that they *wouldn't*.

God is calling us to higher living. When He leads us to the intersection of destiny and decision, He simply asks His child to trust Him, to take that next step of faith, and to buy the field. I like the counsel one author gave concerning the decision to act.

> There's nothing noble about an unlived life you thought of living. There's nothing romantic about audacious, unrealized dreams. Nothing honorable about sacrifices made begrudgingly for a life you end up resenting. If you want to be something, why not begin by doing it? If you long to be a writer, then write. If an actor, then act. And if a runner, run. This is what determines all great endeavors—not just another interesting idea to talk about a coffee shop, but the decision to act, to move. One small step after another.[1]

The clock is ticking with all the hosts of Heaven looking on. So very much hangs in the balance of your decision. Don't allow procrastination and neglect to steal your life's calling. Count the cost. Pay the price. Buy the field. Do it now.

BLUE LIGHTS AND BLACK FRIDAYS

The summer following my freshman year of college, I took a summer job at the K-Mart in Bay City, Texas. This was a small, insignificant store in likewise a small, insignificant town. It was a no-frills K-mart, not some BigK monstrosity where square footage measures into the six digit range. There were no self-checkout stations with handy-dandy touch screens. There were a total of three checkout registers. Although some products did have bar codes incorporated into their packaging back then, minimum wage earning plebes, such as myself, had no clue what they were for, and we certainly had nothing to scan them with at the register. Whatever the price was on the sticker was what we rang it up for.

For the handful of customers who paid by credit card, it was an enormous time sink. The checker would have to pull out a paper printout of the credit card industry's version of Santa's naughty list and make sure that the name on their photo ID was nowhere to be found on Visa or MasterCard's *Most Wanted*. Then, we had to get out the credit card swipe machine and the carbon copy paper form. We swiped the card and had the customer write on the bottom of the slip their driver's license number, Social Security number, and phone number. Amidst the backdrop of today's technology advances, the whole clumsy scene appears more than a little bit backwoods.

But, we did have one thing that no BigK, Hyper-Walmart, Meijer, or Super-Target of today could in good conscious boast—that's right, the one and only blue light special. The allure of the blue light special was all the more persuasive because it was backed by the three most famous words known to man during that day. No, not, "I Love You," "Seize the Day," "Pass the Biscuits," or even "Praise the Lord." Nope. Throughout the decade that was the 80s, the three recognized words were, "Attention K-mart shoppers." When patrons of K-mart heard that sound, it only meant one thing. Somewhere within the hallowed halls of the store, a deal was to be found. The item over which the blue light loomed large was for the most part inconsequential. Perhaps it was half-off all discontinued inventory of pet rocks, or two dashboard bobble head Chihuahuas for a buck. Perhaps it was BOGO Chia Pet hippopotamus while supplies lasted. Regardless, when the blue siren was boldly flashing for all the world to see (or at least all the store) and those three infamous words rippled like echoing thunder throughout the corridors of K-Mart, it was on.

Granted, that was the 80s and much has changed in the years since. Blue light specials have come and gone and given way to Black Friday (which is pretty much a sleep-deprived, day-long version of the blue light special across the entire retail marketplace). Ours is the culture ever in trivial pursuit of a deal. But when it comes to finding and fulfilling God's will for your life, there are no flashing blue sirens, door busters, or early bird specials. God's will and His best for your life can never be found at rock-bottom discounted prices. No clearance tags will ever dangle from something so precious.

DEAL OR NO DEAL

To follow the will of God for our life is a monumental, life-long adventure. It's no small wonder that Jesus gave a cautionary message before embarking upon such a noble quest.

> *For which of you, intending to build a tower, sitteth not down first, and counteth the cost, whether he have sufficient to finish it? Lest haply, after he hath laid the foundation, and is not able to finish it, all that behold*

it begin to mock him, Saying, This man began to build,
and was not able to finish. —LUKE 14:28–30

This something-for-nothing mindset which permeates present-day thinking is foreign to the legends in Scripture that made their lives count for the glory of God. In the aftermath of King David's undiscerning census, seventy-thousand valiant men of Israel fell to pestilence in a single day. To bring an end to the plague, the Lord instructed David to erect an altar that would serve as both a reminder to the consequences of man's sin and also the goodness of God in His deliverance.

As a king, David owned vast holdings including much land. God could have instructed him to break ground on any spot of thousands of acres which either he or the nation of Israel already held in their possession. But through the prophet Gad, the Lord instructed David to set up this altar at the spot where the angel of the Lord had appeared. That location was a threshing floor that belonged to Ornan, a Jebusite man.

Then David said to Ornan, Grant me the place of
this threshingfloor, that I may build an altar therein
unto the LORD: thou shalt grant it me for the full
price: that the plague may be stayed from the people.
And Ornan said unto David, Take it to thee, and let
my lord the king do that which is good in his eyes:
lo, I give thee the oxen also for burnt offerings, and
the threshing instruments for wood, and the wheat
for the meat offering; I give it all. And king David
said to Ornan, Nay; but I will verily buy it for the

full price: for I will not take that which is thine for
the LORD, nor offer burnt offerings without cost.
—1 CHRONICLES 21:22–24

Did you catch it? With the most noble of intentions, Ornan essentially says, "David, your money is no good here. What's mine is yours. You want to buy my place and offer a sacrifice to God? Well I am prepared to make you an offer that you simply can't refuse. As a gift, no strings attached, I want to give you this threshing floor and all that you see. In fact, I have a prize bullock out grazing on the back forty that the Mrs. and I were going to butcher next week, but you can have it for your sacrifice. But wait, that's not all; I'll even throw in all these threshing instruments which will make great kindling wood to light the fires upon which your sacrifice will be offered."

To this well-meant gesture of generosity, David looks at Ornan and sternly states, "Thanks, but no thanks." David would not accept such generosity. More to the point, he could not in good conscience offer up something to God as a sacrifice which cost him absolutely nothing.

What a striking contrast to the, you-won't-believe-the-deal-I-got mindset! Utilizing such contemporary negotiating tactics, David would have been better served by telling Ornan that his price wasn't even in the ballpark. David could have acted coy, sending the message that there were no less than half a dozen other prominent, more favorable sites that are currently in his consideration mix. David could have been wise for his countenance to signal a rather disinterested, unimpressed posture in the property which Ornan held the title deed to. Instead, he was transparent. His approach was "this is the property God told me to get; therefore, this is the property I want and will pay top dollar for, nothing less, nothing else." End of discussion. David was keen that this threshing floor was God's will, and as such, he knew that there is always a cost to be counted and a price to be paid.

What David could not have possibly known was that there was more at stake than what met the eye. The site of Ornan's threshing floor was strategic in God's plan for His people. It was situated high upon Mount Moriah. Long before this parcel of land was to be employed in the threshing of wheat, it was a place of sacrifice believed to have been the exact site where Abraham offered his son Isaac to the Lord as a burnt sacrifice (a foreshadowing of the once-and-for-all sacrifice for sin that God the Father would make through His Son, Jesus Christ). Again and again in Scripture, there is a connection between Moriah and this matter of sacrifice. This was not the first, nor would it be the last, altar to be built on this site. David's son Solomon would hold a ribbon cutting ceremony to end all such ceremonies on this same sacred parcel of land in the dedication ceremony for Solomon's newly constructed Temple. *"Then Solomon began to build the house of the LORD at Jerusalem in mount Moriah, where the LORD appeared unto David his father, in the place that David had prepared in the threshingfloor of Ornan the Jebusite"* (2 Chronicles 3:1). Are you beginning to link together some of the many moving parts here and connect the dots? No? Read on. (If yes, please read on, too!)

If all of those prior linkages were not eyebrow raising enough, this same square footage in present day Jerusalem will also be the site where demolition crews will one day roll in, reduce the Mosque of Omar (a.k.a., the Dome of the Rock) to rubble. This will pave the way for the construction of the third temple to be built during the not-so-distant future period commonly referred to as the tribulation period.

With all of this in mind, we can now begin to see how a flashing blue light situated prominently above the entrance to Ornan's threshing floor would mitigate the sacred nature of what had previously taken place, what is taking place presently, and what will one day take place prophetically. In the midst of it all, David couldn't possibly see the totality of what was on the line. Sure he was able to put the pieces together with how this one wrong, through disobedience, would forever impact seventy thousand men and their grieving families. He could not have fathomed how that one wrong made right through obedience, was instrumental to what God was orchestrating and would forever benefit and impact countless others. By the way, neither could Will Borden, or hundreds of other heroes of the faith whose names and stories of service and surrender to the Lord Jesus Christ could be inserted here.

Feel a bit like it is your vision that is impaired and that you can't see the beginning from the end? Dumbfounded as to why God is prompting you to take to heart the plea of the great hymn "Trust and Obey"? Speechless that He desires the words of that chorus to leap out at you from the hymnal pages, wooing you to live it out each and every day of the week? Pick your head up—you're in good company. Perhaps those waiting on the other end of your obedience are just as numerous as those who were doing likewise as David came to the great crossroads in his life. Let's bring an end to the domineering stalemate that has placed shackles on your life— trust and obey God come what may. Step out and buy the field once and for all.

PART TWO

FOLLOW GOD'S CALL

Follow the grain in your own wood.—**Howard Thurman**

A man is not old until regrets take the place of dreams.
—John Barrymore

*Too many people are thinking of security instead of opportunity.
They seem more afraid of life than death.*—**James F. Byrnes**

*The great thing in this world is not so much where you stand, as
in what direction you are moving.*—**Oliver Wendell Holmes**

CHAPTER FIVE

WORK THE FIELD

*She considereth a field, and buyeth it: with
the fruit of her hands she planteth a vineyard.*
—Proverbs 31:16

For Korean fisherman Kim Yong-Chul, a day in July of 2007 started off like most any other. He made his way from his house to the harbor in the small fishing village of Taean, some sixty miles southwest of the capitol city of Seoul. He climbed aboard his fishing vessel, made ready the nets, hoisted the anchor, and set sail into the Yellow Sea. He was hoping for a great haul of Webfoot Octopus. While it may not exactly make mouths water for us westerners, the unwieldy sea creature is considered a gourmet delicacy in Korea and select countries throughout the eastern Pacific Rim.

Yong-Chul's hopes were realized as he did in fact haul in such a marine animal, but he pulled up far more from the depths of the Yellow Sea that fateful day. Attached to the octopus' tentacles were shards of antique pottery. Between what he brought up in his nets that day and subsequent dive expositions, some thirty bowls would be recovered. His treasure dated back to the twelfth century, during the period when the Koryo Dynasty ruled over the Korean peninsula. One fisherman's ordinary day "at the office" proved to be extraordinary and is hailed as one of the great undersea discoveries of modern times.

JUST ANOTHER DAY IN THE LIFE OF _____

For Kim Yong-Chul, the day-in and day-out faithfulness of working his field had, in the most unsuspecting of moments, an immense payday. Our reward for steady commitment to working in the field God has for us is not something that makes headline news, nor is it likely to produce great wealth and fame overnight. Incredible life rewards, both of the tangible and intangible variety, await the diligent worker who each day faithfully rolls up his sleeves, not afraid to get dirt under his fingernails, and labors in his Father's field.

Migrant farm workers, who go from place to place in search of seasonal work, have jobs that are often rather uninspiring because of the hard work, long hours, and relatively low pay. But the God, who beckons us to, *"Take my yoke upon you…For my yoke is easy, and my burden is light"*

(Matthew 11:29–30), is no such taskmaster. He is a God that will be indebted to no man and faithfully rewards those who labor for Him. What kind of rewards? Well, Paul writes about our laboring in the field for Christ in his first letter to the church at Corinth.

> *I have planted, Apollos watered; but God gave the increase. So then neither is he that planteth any thing, neither he that watereth; but God that giveth the increase. Now he that planteth and he that watereth are one: and every man shall receive his own reward according to his own labour. For we are labourers together with God: ye are God's husbandry, ye are God's building. According to the grace of God which is given unto me...* —1 CORINTHIANS 3:6–10

From this one account, let us consider six rewards for faithfulness in our field.

Reward #1: Expending Ourselves for God's Glory

I have planted—1 CORINTHIANS 3:6A

It has been stated that this world is full of willing people— some willing to work, and others willing to let them. It is both exhilarating and exhausting to serve the Lord with all of our heart, soul, and mind as the Scriptures command us to do. We wake up each morning with the same opportunity to use the day in service to God or a far less lofty aim. It seems the familiar statement really is true: "Only two choices on the shelf; serving God or serving self." In theory, we know that serving God pays dividends in the sweet bye-and-bye, but practically, serving ourselves beckons us with an immediate payout in the nasty here and now. Serving God appears, on the surface, to require a whole lot more heavy lifting than serving self requires. Yet isn't that how most once-in-a-lifetime opportunities usually make entrance in our lives, ever so cleverly disguised as hard work? *"But let every man prove his own work, and then shall he have rejoicing in himself alone, and not in another. For every man shall bear his own burden"* (Galatians 6:4–5). No man can ride the coattails of another man's experience of salvation, and so it is with one's service.

Reward #2: Seeing God Multiply Our Efforts

But God gave the increase—1 CORINTHIANS 3:6B

The farmer tills the land, balances soil nutrition, plants the field, watches the weather forecasts, applies crop protection chemicals, irrigates, and more. He does everything within his power to enable his field to yield a bumper crop. There are still many variables outside his control, highly influential factors such as weather temperatures and precipitation. There are no guarantees, as the psalmist reminds us, *"And sow the fields, and plant vineyards, which may yield fruits of increase"* (Psalms 107:37). In His timing and in accordance with His will, it delights God to bless and multiply our diligent efforts for His glory.

Reward #3: Knowing Our Place

I have planted, Apollos watered; but God gave the increase. So then neither is he that planteth any thing, neither he that watereth; but God that giveth the increase.—1 CORINTHIANS 3:6–7

Our job is to work the work He has called us to do. The final tally on such labors is up to Him. *"Faithful is he that calleth you, who also will do it"* (1 Thessalonians 5:24). We would do well to heed the counsel, "Work as if it all depended on you; pray as if it all depended on God." That is our role—our place. If we are not guarded, we can buy into the lies which Satan whispers and our flesh quickly acquiesces to. We must turn a deaf ear toward Satan's enticing, deceitful words and allow Scripture to bend our ear, *"For if a man think himself to be something, when he is nothing, he deceiveth himself"* (Galatians 6:3). Do not be deceived friend. Verses six and seven above in 1 Corinthians 3 remind us that on our own, we are nothing.

Whether in the classroom, workplace, athletic court, or even our own self-imposed expectations, we live in a world where there is constant pressure to perform. What a wonderful blessing to know that in God's harvest field, our call is one of remaining faithful and working and serving Him in humility. *"By humility and the fear of the LORD are riches, and honour, and life"* (Proverbs 22:4). Only then can we confidently leave the results of such love-driven labor in His hands.

Reward #4: Serving alongside Others

Now he that planteth and he that watereth are one.
—1 CORINTHIANS 3:8A

I haven't always been a pastor. The recognition of my call came later in life. The decade following my college graduation, I had an amazing job with a world-leading pharmaceutical company, which also had a division that manufactured turf protection products such as insecticides and fungicides. For the first half of those ten years, I worked in sales and visited superintendents at golf courses in an effort to inform them of our products and help evaluate whether they had a fit within the superintendent's turf management program. (Yep, I always traveled from course to course with my golf clubs in the back of the company car—jealous much?)

Many golf courses have a particular turf grass species called bent grass on their greens, tees, and often fairways. Golf course superintendents are paid to maintain the turf conditions to the highest standards. As one integral part of that effort, they must tackle different turf grass diseases that threaten the overall health and vigor of the turf.

During my time in this field, there was an emerging disease pathogen complex that attacked bent grass, referred to as summer bent grass decline. There was no single product that was successful in suppressing the pathogen. Superintendents did what they could from a soil management perspective (closely managing fertility, altering watering practices, raising mowing heights, and adding soil amendments) to keep their turf healthy through those times of high plant stress. This was all that could be done.

Through research sponsored by university and manufacturers, a combination of two active ingredients, Mancozeb and Fosetyl-Al, proved to be highly effective. These products were made by two multi-billion dollar global corporations who competed fiercely against each other in other markets. Yet they collectively worked together and seized the opportunity in this segment. Alone, their products were both largely ineffective against summer bent grass decline, but together, there was synergy. Conventional wisdom holds that 1+1=2, but in a synergistic setting, 1+1=3, the collective sum is greater than the individual parts. These two companies partnered, did a lot in the way of co-marketing the two products, and won. The customer won. Hey, the grass even won! Everyone but the disease pathogen (and competing companies) came out the better for it. Why? Because they locked arms and worked together.

That spirit of oneness and working together is how God intended for it to be in our Christian life, *"Stand fast in one spirit, with one mind striving together for the faith of the gospel"* (Philippians 1:27). Within the church, God has given individuals unique gifts. *"And he gave some, apostles; and some, prophets; and some, evangelists; and some, pastors and teachers; For the perfecting of the saints, for the work of the ministry, for the edifying of the body of Christ"* (Ephesians 4:11–12). When working in isolation, these gifts will not live up to their potential and have impact for the cause of Christ and in the lives of others. But, laboring together alongside fellow Christians in local churches, there is synergy and unconventional math, whose equation could be best expressed as 1+1 =3.

Reward #5: Equity

And every man shall receive his own reward according to his own labour—1 CORINTHIANS 3:8B

We live in an unfair world. Lawlessness abounds, and sometimes those who are wicked and do evil seem to get overlooked by authorities, while people striving to do right can appear at times to be overlooked by God. The prophet Isaiah described this well when he penned: *"And judgment is turned away backward, and justice standeth afar off: for truth is fallen in the street, and equity cannot enter"* (Isaiah 59:14).

First Corinthians 3:8 reminds us that there will come a day when all things inequitable will come to a halt, for *"Every man shall receive his own reward according to his own labour."* We have the assurance from Scripture, *"I will render to the man according to his work"* (Proverbs 24:29). This day of reckoning and the establishment of equity is described in the parable of the talents.

*After a long time the lord of those servants cometh, and reckoneth with them. And so he that had received five talents came and brought other five talents, saying, Lord, thou deliveredst unto me five talents: behold, I have gained beside them five talents more. His lord said unto him, Well done, thou good and faithful servant: thou hast been faithful over a few things, I will make thee ruler over many things: enter thou into the joy of thy lord. He also that had received two talents came and said, Lord, thou deliveredst unto me two talents: behold, I have gained two other talents beside them. His lord said unto him, Well done, good and faithful servant; thou hast been faithful over a few things, I will make thee ruler over many things: enter thou into the joy of thy lord. Then he which had received the one talent came and said, Lord, I knew thee that thou art an hard man, reaping where thou hast not sown, and gathering where thou hast not strawed: And I was afraid, and went and hid thy talent in the earth: lo, there thou hast that is thine. His lord answered and said unto him, Thou wicked and slothful servant, thou knewest that I reap where I sowed not, and gather where I have not strawed: Thou oughtest therefore to have put my money to the exchangers, and then at my coming I should have received mine own with usury. Take therefore the talent from him, and give it unto him which hath ten talents.—*MATTHEW 25:19–28

In this account, Jesus compares the kingdom of Heaven with a man who went on a long journey. Before he did, he called in three of his servants and gave one five talents, another two talents, and the third servant one talent. The man with the five talents and the one with the two were good stewards and wise in their dealings. They doubled their money. Unfortunately, the man that was given one talent did nothing with it. He chose to bury it in the dirt. He had to stand before his master and give account of his doings, as will every one of us.

Reward #6: Working With God.

For we are labourers together with God.
—1 CORINTHIANS 3:9A

The final reward is an overwhelming one to meditate upon. By being diligent in working our field, we have joined forces with the Creator of the universe. What an amazing thought! The invitation to labor together is open to all, as Jesus said, *"The harvest truly is plenteous, but the labourers are few; Pray ye therefore the Lord of the harvest, that he will send forth labourers into his harvest"* (Matthew 9:37–38). We need to be reminded from time to time that, together, God and I make a majority, and He can do anything. Now, that is synergy that blows the lid off of 1+1=2. That's more like 1+1=INFINITY.

Regardless of the vocational field, God rewards His faithful servants handsomely. He places great value on work, for God Himself is a worker. We see this reality from the earliest chapters of the Bible.

> *And on the seventh day God ended his work which he had made; and he rested on the seventh day from all his work which he had made. And God blessed the seventh day, and sanctified it: because that in it he had rested from all his work which God created and made.*—GENESIS 2:2–3

Some are under the faulty assumption that work is a result of the curse from the fall of Adam. But before the fall, Adam had a 9–5 job with the best work commute views ever. He was commissioned from God to work in Eden. *"And the LORD God took the man, and put him into the garden of Eden to dress it and to keep it"* (Genesis 2:15). Jesus Himself weighed in on the high calling of work with these words, *"I must work the works of him that sent me, while it is day: the night cometh, when no man can work"* (John 9:4). Regardless of the particular field, to be Christ-like is to be a worker. What a joy and great reward it brings when we partner with Christ in His work and are co-laborers with Him.

CONSERVATION RESERVE PROGRAM

The Conservation Reserve Program, or CRP as it is better known in rural America, is a long-standing program with the aim of reducing topsoil erosion. In so doing, it conserves one of our greatest natural resources: our nation's farmland. CRP offers numerous upsides, such as the reduction of water runoff and sedimentation, thereby offering heightened protection to our groundwater, lakes, rivers, ponds, and streams. The program is certainly favorable for wildlife, as millions of acres of tillable land are set aside, allowing for ground cover establishment that serves as a welcomed habitat for outdoor critters of most every shape and size. It also can have an appreciable impact on the American farmer. By taking tillable land out of production that was once used to grow crops such as corn, soybeans and wheat, CRP helps keep the bottom from falling out of grain commodity prices.

Of course, like many other forms of governmental assistance programs, CRP also carries the potential for abuse. On a practical level, one of the unfavorable aspects of the well-intended program is that it issues payments to landowners for *not* working the land.

Although CRP for America's farmers and landowners has its merits, no such subsidy program exists within the framework of God's economy. If we refuse to roll up our sleeves and answer the call, or go about our work in the field half-heartedly and lacking in zeal, then that too has its own reward. *"I went by the field of the slothful…And, lo, it was all grown over with thorns, and nettles had covered the face thereof, and the stone wall thereof was broken down"* (Proverbs 24:30–31). We are called to diligently work in our field as long as we live.

"In the sweat of thy face shalt thou eat bread, till thou return unto the ground" (Genesis 3:19A).

With sweat and toil come the sweet rewards of laboring in obedience to God: *"The sleep of a labouring man is sweet, whether he eat little or much"* (Ecclesiastes 5:12). You may have never woken up in the morning on a SleepNumber bed, nor can you boast of a Tempur-Pedic mattress in the master suite, but work your field just the same, Christian. Sleep well.

It's never too late to be who you might have been.—**George Eliot**

Even when opportunity knocks, a man still has to get up off his seat and open the door.—**Anonymous**

Many an opportunity is lost because a man is out looking for four-leaf clovers.—**Anonymous**

CHAPTER SIX

PAY FOR THE FIELD

For which of you, intending to build a tower, sitteth
not down first, and counteth the cost, whether he have
sufficient to finish it? Lest haply, after he hath laid the
foundation, and is not able to finish it, all that behold
it begin to mock him, Saying, This man began to build,
and was not able to finish.—LUKE 14:28–30

North Korean government officials would have been wise to take the verse above to heart before breaking ground on the Ryugyong Hotel. Esquire magazine dubbed it "the worst building in the history of mankind." The Ryugyong Hotel (aka, the hotel of doom, the phantom hotel, the tower of terror, and a myriad of other unflattering titles) is a towering, empty, concrete shell that was once intended to be a hotel in Pyongyang, the capitol and largest city in the country. It reaches a massive height of 105 stories (just five stories short of the former World Trade Center Towers) and reportedly encompasses nearly four million square feet—a staggering ninety acres under one roof. Architectural plans called for eight rotating floors and seven revolving restaurants, perched high above the gargantuan hotel's three thousand plus vacant rooms.

All of this serves to make The Ryugyong the largest hotel in the world that you will likely never receive a wake-up call from the front desk in, order room service from, or so much as go for a ride on the elevator in. This is due to three reasons. First, vacation travel to communist North Korea is highly restricted. Second, in an effort to keep costs in check, it was rumored that suspect concrete was used, calling into question the safety and integrity of the overall structure. And third, construction that began on the pyramid-shaped hotel in 1987 abruptly stopped in 1992 and would lay dormant for the next nearly sixteen years due to insufficient funds.

The estimated cost of the hotel back in the mid '80s represented about 2 percent of North Korea's entire Gross National Product (GNP). Seems a little lavish, especially for a city (and a country) that is not on anyone's short list for a road trip. Clearly, someone was negligent in sitting down and counting the cost. Although construction has resumed in recent years, NSF (Non-Sufficient Funds) is stamped firmly on the permanent record of the Ryugyong Hotel. Those three letters might as well be rubber stamped diagonally in ninety-six point, cherry red font across every photo, postcard, or desktop wallpaper in existence of the Ryugyong Hotel. In a dismal effort to salve their conscience for much of the last two decades, North Korean officials have edited the phantom hotel out of their city skyline photos before publishing. This is much the equivalent as when our one-year-old daughter sat on my lap and placed her hands over her eyes, smugly confident that she was now cleverly concealed from view and that Daddy could no longer see her!

None of us want to fall into the NSF trap that North Korea did, as they failed to count the costs upfront. Nor would it be honest for us to airbrush over the ruins of failed attempts, relationships, and a myriad of other empty endeavors that came up short from the landscape of our lives. What steps can we take to minimize the likelihood of having NSF stamped across the field of our dreams? We all are aware there are no guarantees in life, but there are those things we can do to ensure we have what it takes to not only buy the field but also have the means to pay for it.

CASH OR CREDIT OR...?

Google Wallet, Square, Apple Pay, PayPal, and other such payments have revolutionized online purchasing behaviors. Membership has its privileges at American Express, and who could argue that Visa is everywhere you want to be? But there are no electronic credit card swipe machines located nearby God's field for you. Payment in the form of a personal check is not on the short list of legal tender. MasterCard's ad slogan rings true, "There are some things that money cannot buy; for everything else, there's MasterCard." The field of God's plan for your life falls into the category of things that money cannot buy. While "Life takes Visa," the procurement of your field most definitely does not.

So if it's not credit cards or cash, exactly what kind of currency puts a SOLD sticker triumphantly across the For Sale By Owner sign out in your field? Matthew 13:44 gives us some profound insights to the answer to this question and the unconventional, unconditional, medium of exchange that is required. *"Again, the kingdom of heaven is like unto treasure hid in a field; the which when a man hath found, he hideth, and for joy thereof goeth and selleth all that he hath, and buyeth that field."* Let's dissect this verse into smaller parcels, for within it we have a template for anyone who is committed to buying and paying for their field.

CURRENCY #1: DILIGENCE

Matthew 13:44 is a fitting monument to the life's work of diligent hands. In the workplace, no character trait is more esteemed, or in shorter supply, than that of diligence. Diligence can always be found in someone dead-set on making a difference for others. Diligence is often the tipping point between excellence and mediocrity, success and failure, wealth and poverty, leading and following, thriving and surviving, and between NSF and paid in full.

There is a biblical law of sowing and reaping put forth in Scripture.

Be not deceived; God is not mocked: for whatsoever a man soweth, that shall he also reap. For he that soweth to his flesh shall of the flesh reap corruption; but he that soweth to the Spirit shall of the Spirit reap life everlasting. And let us not be weary in well doing: for in due season we shall reap, if we faint not.
—Galatians 6:7–9

The diligent soul that time and again shakes off weariness in well doing, has a beautiful, bountiful harvest awaiting to be reaped by him. Concerning the yield of diligence, A.W. Tozer once remarked, "The result of diligence is a faith that is strong and willing to inherit the fulfillment of the promises of God." The following are a few of the other great and desirous things that diligence reaps in the Christian life.

In due season diligence reaps FINANCIAL SECURITY.

"*He becometh poor that dealeth with a slack hand: but the hand of the diligent maketh rich*" (Proverbs 10:4). Everyone wants lasting financial security, but it is the diligent who are going to know it up close and personal for themselves.

In due season diligence reaps AUTHORITY.

"*The hand of the diligent shall bear rule: but the slothful shall be under tribute*" (Proverbs 12:24). An industrious person that sticks to his work daily will be held in honor and advance in positions of responsibility and authority. "*And the man Jeroboam was a mighty man of valour: and Solomon seeing the young man that he was industrious, he made him ruler over all the charge of the house of Joseph"* (1 Kings 11:28). This principle rings true not only in this present life, but also in eternal life. *"His lord said unto him, Well done, thou good and faithful servant: thou hast been faithful over a few things, I will make thee ruler over many things: enter thou into the joy of thy lord"* (Matthew 25:21).

Referred to often as the *Prince of Preachers,* Charles Spurgeon was a Baptist Pastor from the late nineteeth century. In one of his many stirring literary works, *John Ploughman's Talk,* Spurgeon offers page after page of practical wisdom and insights, at times employing satire to make a point. Notice this little gem about the one who lacks diligence and is given over to laziness.

> Every man ought to have patience and pity for poverty; but for laziness, a long whip, or a turn at the treadmill might be better. This would be healthy physic for all sluggards; but there is no chance of some of them getting their full dose of this medicine, for they were born with silver spoons in their mouths, and like spoons, they will scarce stir their own tea unless somebody lends them a hand. They are, as the old proverb says, "as lazy as Ludham's dog, that leaned his head against the wall to bark"; and, like lazy sheep, it is too much trouble for them to carry their own wool[1]…a man who wastes his time and his strength in sloth offers himself to be a good target for the devil, who is a wonderfully good rifleman, and will riddle the idler with his shots; in other words, idle men tempt the devil to tempt them. He who plays when he

should work, has an evil spirit to be his playmate; and he who neither works nor plays is a workshop for Satan. If the devil catch a man idle, he will set him to work, find him tools, and before long pay him wages[2]…My advice to my boys has always been, get out of the sluggard's way, or you may catch his disease, and never rid of it. I am always afraid of learning the ways of the idle, and am very watchful to nip anything of the sort in the bud; for you know it is best to kill the lion while it is a cub.[3]

This is the self-created portion of the one who has succumbed to idleness. Those given to industry, in due season, will reap the desirable fruit of authority.

In due season diligence reaps ABUNDANCE.

"The soul of the sluggard desireth, and hath nothing: but the soul of the diligent shall be made fat" (Proverbs 13:4). *Fat* carries the idea of abounding in provisions—never lacking necessity and always having more than enough. I believe in the motivating power of having a dream—a vision for our life. But sitting around daydreaming does nothing to conjoin the dreamer with his dream. It has been said, "No dream ever comes true, until you wake up and go to work." Wishful thinking is perhaps the poorest and most unprofitable of all substitutes for hard work. Yet so many seem bent on making the trade. The sluggard is covetous of that which he does not have and envious of those who have it. Yet he is unwilling to do anything of his own volition to work and go after it.

In due season diligence reaps SUCCESS.

"He that diligently seeketh good procureth favour" (Proverbs 11:27). Motivational speaker Anthony Robbins put it succinctly: "The meeting of preparation with opportunity generates the offspring we call luck." Whatever name you want to give it, luck, chance, or fortune always will be on the side of the diligent. Diligent people seem to be the luckiest souls on the earth, but there is nothing lucky about their situation. They have procured it for themselves by much diligence.

In due season diligence reaps GRATEFULNESS.

"The slothful man roasteth not that which he took in hunting: but the substance of a diligent man is precious" (Proverbs 12:27). A sure way to lose what you have is to allow a sense of entitlement to take up residence in your thought life. Slothfulness reaps an ungrateful spirit toward others around you as well as toward God and His provisions. Diligent men and women are full of gratitude. They do not have the time or interest in musing on such unprofitable thinking.

In due season diligence reaps SOUND THINKING.

"The thoughts of the diligent tend only to plenteousness; but of every one that is hasty only to want" (Proverbs 21:5). While it may not be on the radar of the Center for Disease Control and Prevention, procrastination, laziness, and an entitlement-driven mentality have nearly reached epidemic status in today's

culture. In contrast, diligent people have sound thinking. When you daily strive to cultivate diligence in all that you do, you will find a completely unexpected, but welcomed by-product. Your mind will be more creative, optimistic, and full of ideas and possibilities—all of which will motivate you. God blesses and rewards our endeavors when we make our minds up to honor these biblical precepts.

In due season diligence reaps ADVANCEMENT.

"Seest thou a man diligent in his business? he shall stand before kings; he shall not stand before mean men" (Proverbs 22:29). *Mean men* is not a description for unkind, wicked men but common, ho-hum, run-of-the-mill, average individuals.

In due season, the diligent man finds his way near the top. In the feeblest of schemes to get noticed, the slothful have enslaved themselves to the ball of regret and the chain of all that might have been in their lives. I like what Benjamin Franklin said: "Diligence overcomes difficulties; sloth makes them." Diligence in your labor gains the attention of people who are in powerful positions. Look at the biblical accounts of Joseph, Jeroboam, and Daniel—a few diligent folks in Scripture—and the advancement that came their way as a result of their diligence.

Diligence is a powerful, universally accepted form of currency. It will take you anywhere you want to be. When buying the field, don't leave home without it.

THE CURRENCY OF DISCERNMENT

...the which, when a man hath found...

The game *Hot-Warm-Cold* is sort of a twist on the classic, *Hide-n-Go-Seek*. One person simply hides an object and calls for the other person to come and try to, as we say in the country, birddog it. The one who hid the object will give the person clues of a thermal nature as to their nearness in finding the hidden object. For instance, if the person was not anywhere in close proximity, the other might say, "You're cold. Freezing cold. You're like ice!" Then as the person makes their way in the direction that they should go, they might hear counsel such as, "You're getting warmer. Warmer. Warmer. Hot. You're getting hot. You're burning up! Dude, you're like on fire!" I am sure the game has its variations from one part of the country to the next, but you get the gist.

One of the funny and frequent aspects of the game is when someone who is *on fire* is standing right by what they are looking for, yet they fail to see it. If they were any closer, it would reach out and bite them, and they still cannot seem to spot it. Similarly, one of the frequent, but not nearly so hilarious aspects to life, is when someone is so very close to living the life they imagined for God's glory. They are within such proximity to unearthing God's calling upon their life, yet because of a lack in discernment, they fail to discover it. This is why our passage says *"The which when a man hath found...."* It takes discernment to *find* it.

Three principal reasons could be cited as to why we come up short in the discernment department and miss those God appointed opportunities to buy the field:

We are only looking for fireworks.

I love walking through grocery stores on sample day. Not only does the store make delicious food available, but, at least where I live, the sample givers take their job seriously and practically insist you try their product. From one aisle to the next, everywhere you turn, someone will wave you down to get your attention and almost accost you with offerings of delectable samplings.

We can unfairly expect opportunities to be presented in much the same manner as samples at the supermarket. We anticipate destiny to be vying for our eye-level attention at every turn. We want fate to be served up hot and fresh on a silver platter almost everywhere that we are. Generally speaking, however, that's just no how it works.

There are exceptions, as the Old Testament describes one account of just how obvious the Lord was leading and guiding His children from Egypt to the promise land.

> *And the* Lord *went before them by day in a pillar of a cloud, to lead them the way; and by night in a pillar of fire, to give them light; to go by day and night: He took not away the pillar of the cloud by day, nor the pillar of fire by night, from before the people.*
> —Exodus 13:21–22

I suppose there are those rarest of Christian men and women who could give a testimony that God clearly spoke to them in a *burning bush* type manner. Praise God, when He chooses to do such. Most of us would bear witness that God opens up doors of opportunity to buy and pay for the field in a far subtler, less obvious fashion. Someone noted, "Opportunities? They are all around us. There is power lying latent everywhere waiting for the observant eye to discover it." While there are noteworthy exceptions, the complete absence of fanfare is likewise the prominent pattern from Scripture of how God leads and guides. Scripture describes God's guidance as available for those who will listen to God's still small voice, not as coming by way of lighting bolt.

> *I will instruct thee and teach thee in the way which thou shalt go: I will guide thee with mine eye.*
> —PSALMS 32:8

> *Trust in the LORD with all thine heart; and lean not unto thine own understanding. In all thy ways acknowledge him, and he shall direct thy paths.*
> —PROVERBS 3:5–6

> *…And, behold, the LORD passed by, and a great and strong wind rent the mountains, and brake in pieces the rocks before the LORD; but the LORD was not in the wind: and after the wind an earthquake; but the LORD was not in the earthquake: And after the earthquake a fire; but the LORD was not in the fire: and after the fire a still small voice. And it was so, when Elijah heard it,*

that he wrapped his face in his mantle, and went out,
and stood in the entering in of the cave. And, behold,
there came a voice unto him, and said, What doest
thou here, Elijah?—1 KINGS 19:11–13

Opportunities to buy the field are all around us. You'll miss it altogether if you expect it to show up at your doorstep decked out with flashy accessories amidst exploding fireworks. No, opportunity almost always makes its presence quietly known alongside us in the routines of everyday life.

We fail to ask.

Of all the regrettable reasons to let an opportunity slip, this perhaps is the most tragic. What an unacceptable reason to be negligent towards a God-appointed opportunity. James 4:2 tells us, "...*ye have not, because ye ask not.*" And James 1:5 offers, "*If any of you lack wisdom, let him ask of God, that giveth to all men liberally, and upbraideth not; and it shall be given him.*"

You're roughly half way through reading this book. If you haven't already paused along the way to ask God for discernment concerning His field for you, now would be a good time to set the book aside and do exactly that.

This was the first thing a young lady named Achsah did, when she was about to start a new life with Othniel. Scripture records that she approached her father Caleb and asked him for a field. "*And it came to pass, as she came unto him, that she moved him to ask of her father a field: and she lighted off her ass; and Caleb said unto her, What wouldest thou?*"

(Joshua 15:18). When was the last time you posed the same question to your Heavenly Father? God invites you to ask: *"Thus saith the LORD the maker thereof, the LORD that formed it, to establish it; the LORD is his name; Call unto me, and I will answer thee, and shew thee great and mighty things, which thou knowest not"* (Jeremiah 33:2–3). From His throne of grace, our Heavenly Father stands ready, saying to His children, *"What wouldest thou?"*

We are too busy.

One of the prevailing evils of our day that is largely undetected is busyness. Somewhere along the way, far too many have bought into the lie that busyness equates productiveness and that busy people are successful, happy, and fulfilled. Yet in most cases, the correlation is inaccurate. Two solemn accounts from Scripture come to mind, the first being that of Martha. She had the opportunity of a lifetime to enjoy close fellowship with Jesus personally, alive and in the flesh. Yet in her busyness, the opportunity was squandered. Her sister Mary had a to-do list that was every bit as long, yet she resisted the impulse to be hurried and sat at the feet of her Lord.

> *Now it came to pass, as they went, that he entered into a certain village: and a certain woman named Martha received him into her house. And she had a sister called Mary, which also sat at Jesus' feet, and heard his word. But Martha was cumbered about much serving, and came to him, and said, Lord, dost*

thou not care that my sister hath left me to serve alone? bid her therefore that she help me. And Jesus answered and said unto her, Martha, Martha, thou art careful and troubled about many things: But one thing is needful: and Mary hath chosen that good part, which shall not be taken away from her.—Luke 10:38–42

In our own busyness, by default, we unknowingly make far more decisions for ourselves (and for others closest to us) than we could ever imagine.

The second reminder of the remorseful byproduct of busyness is found in the book of 1 Kings.

And as the king passed by, he cried unto the king: and he said, Thy servant went out into the midst of the battle; and, behold, a man turned aside, and brought a man unto me, and said, Keep this man: if by any means he be missing, then shall thy life be for his life, or else thou shalt pay a talent of silver. And as thy servant was busy here and there, he was gone. And the king of Israel said unto him, So shall thy judgment be; thyself hast decided it.—1 Kings 20:39–40

Some readers may remember the movie, *The African Queen*, based on the book by C.S. Forester. The author describes at some length the dilapidated old steamboat for which the movie is named. He depicts the laborious exertions required from the skipper to get a sufficient head of steam to get the ship under way. The trouble was that there were too many leaks and too many faulty seams and joints that the power was dissipating into thin air. Only with the greatest of difficulty could the old boat be persuaded to muster up a fraction of her original power. Its force was diluted by erosion and neglect. The steam oozed out in all kinds of ways, instead of being channeled to thrust with single-minded purpose.

What time and neglect did to the physical make-up of the steamboat, rendering her largely useless is much like the prolonged effect that a lifetime of busyness has on us spiritually. Busyness serves to do not only its sinister work of wearing us down and out; it also keeps us distracted so that we are completely blinded to some amazing opportunities that God has for us. If I could pen 1 Kings 20:40 in the shadow of this truth, it would read something like, "And as the well intentioned Christian was busy here and there, the opportunity was gone."

THE CURRENCY OF DELIGHT

And for joy thereof…

We can do a lot of right things but not necessarily with the right spirit or fueled by the right motivation. Stepping out in faith and buying the field is an awesome, worthwhile adventure for one to devote themselves. If we do so, however, with an embittered or resentful spirit or an aim other than giving Christ the glory due His name, the blessing is forfeited.

Christianity today often comes across as a joyless faith—a marked difference to the faith of the first-century church. What was said of Cain could be likewise said of too many Christians today, *"And Cain was very wroth, and his countenance fell. And the* LORD *said unto Cain, Why art thou wroth? and why is thy countenance fallen?"* (Genesis 4:5–6). We are long overdue to remember that, *"the joy of the* LORD *is your strength"* (Nehemiah 8:10) and to beg God with the prayer, *"The* LORD *lift up his countenance upon thee, and give thee peace"* (Numbers 6:26). We could cry out as David did, *"Restore unto me the joy of thy salvation; and uphold me with thy free spirit"*(Psalm 51:12). This new, unimproved, joyless genre of Christianity today is doing its best in making us weary and is taking its toll on our strength.

If our joyless countenance could be mistaken for the mug shot of Cain, then we need to ask God to help the visage that others see in us more closely resemble the joyful countenance of Caleb. *"But my servant Caleb, because he had another spirit with him, and hath followed me fully, him will I bring into the land whereinto he went; and his seed shall possess it"* (Numbers 14:24). The different spirit of Caleb was certainly one chiefly marked by faith, but I believe that springing from that faith there was a joy that resonated brightly from Caleb's countenance. His joy was evident in his life as a young man and all the way up through his twilight years.

> *Forty years old was I when Moses the servant of the* LORD *sent me from Kadesh-barnea to espy out the land; and I brought him word again as it was in mine heart. Nevertheless my brethren that went up with me made the heart of the people melt: but I wholly*

followed the LORD my God. And Moses sware on that day, saying, Surely the land whereon thy feet have trodden shall be thine inheritance, and thy children's for ever, because thou hast wholly followed the LORD my God. And now, behold, the LORD hath kept me alive, as he said, these forty and five years, even since the LORD spake this word unto Moses, while the children of Israel wandered in the wilderness: and now, lo, I am this day fourscore and five years old. As yet I am as strong this day as I was in the day that Moses sent me: as my strength was then, even so is my strength now, for war, both to go out, and to come in. Now therefore give me this mountain, whereof the LORD spake in that day; for thou heardest in that day how the Anakims were there, and that the cities were great and fenced: if so be the LORD will be with me, then I shall be able to drive them out, as the LORD said.—JOSHUA 14:7–12

The poem below cites the courageous words of Caleb, when he declared to Joshua, "*Now therefore give me this mountain*" (Joshua 14:12). May we too implore the court of Heaven with the mantra, "*Give me this field!*"

Give Me This Mountain
by Shirlee Kimball

*Give me this mountain today, dear Lord; even the peaks
    so high;
Let me lift up mine eyes to the distant hills, as the end of
    the day draws nigh.*

If I linger too long in the valley, dear Lord, I might lose
  the will to go on;
For each hour of the day that I do not climb, makes the
  journey seem harder and long.

Give me this mountain today, dear Lord, while the soft
  breezes blow o'er my soul;
While the sunlight gleams on the distant hills, and I can
  still clearly see my goal.

Give me this mountain today, dear Lord; it's a stepping
  stone to eternal day;
One more mountain, one more hill, Lord; one more step
  on life's way.

THE CURRENCY OF DEDICATION

Goeth and selleth all that he hath…

Paul is a shining example of dedication and single-mindedness in devotion to the cause of Christ.

Not as though I had already attained, either were already perfect: but I follow after, if that I may apprehend that for which also I am apprehended of Christ Jesus. Brethren, I count not myself to have apprehended: but this one thing I do, forgetting those things which are behind, and reaching forth unto those things which are before, I press toward the mark for the prize of the high calling of God in Christ Jesus.
—PHILIPPIANS 3:12–14

Perhaps by now you wonder, "*What is the asking price of the field?*" You're probably thinking, "*Fine, I am going to need discernment, delight, and a healthy dose of diligence, but how much of this dedication thing am I going to have to cough up? I mean, what is the field even listed for sale at anyway? Exactly how much is all of this going to set me back?*" These are fair questions, and you have been more than patient.

So here goes. The non-negotiable list price is (drum roll please)…what the Owner's firm asking price is set at (take a deep breath)…well, the amount someone must give in exchange for the field is (one last pause for effect)…EVERYTHING.

For the man in our Lord's parable to buy the field he had to go and "*selleth all that he hath.*" Friend, it will be no different for you or for me. If you or I were able to buy the field for anything less than our all, the individual in Matthew 13:44 would have a solid case against God for price discrimination.

While *all* is pretty straightforward and easily defined, from person to person and field to field, it can morph a bit. Here are some testimonies of what *all* looked like to a few men and women in Scripture who bought their field.

It cost a poor widow all her livelihood.

And Jesus sat over against the treasury, and beheld how the people cast money into the treasury: and many that were rich cast in much. And there came a certain poor widow, and she threw in two mites, which make a farthing. And he called unto him his disciples, and saith unto them, Verily I say unto you, That this poor widow hath cast more in, than all they which have cast into the treasury: For all they did cast in of their abundance; but she of her want did cast in all that she had, even all her living.—MARK 12:41–44

It cost Paul all that he had once held dear.

But what things were gain to me, those I counted loss for Christ. Yea doubtless, and I count all things but loss for the excellency of the knowledge of Christ Jesus my Lord: for whom I have suffered the loss of all things, and do count them but dung, that I may win Christ.
—PHILIPPIANS 3:7–8

It cost Moses his political ties and riches.

By faith Moses, when he was come to years, refused to be called the son of Pharaoh's daughter; Choosing rather to suffer affliction with the people of God, than to enjoy the pleasures of sin for a season; Esteeming the reproach of Christ greater riches than the treasures in Egypt: for he had respect unto the recompence of the reward.—HEBREWS 11:24–26

It cost the disciples their career paths.

And when they had brought their ships to land, they forsook all, and followed him. —LUKE 5:11

It cost another woman all of her life savings.

> *And being in Bethany in the house of Simon the leper,*
> *as he sat at meat, there came a woman having an*
> *alabaster box of ointment of spikenard very precious;*
> *and she brake the box, and poured it on his head.*
> —MARK 14:3

It cost Jesus His life.

> *Even as the Son of man came not to be ministered*
> *unto, but to minister, and to give his life a ransom for*
> *many.*—MATTHEW 20:28

As Christians, you and I are not exempt from paying the price to follow Christ. "*Verily, verily, I say unto you, The servant is not greater than his lord; neither he that is sent greater than he that sent him*" (John 13:16). The field listing prices have not decreased since the accounts of these men and women from the Bible. But know that when we pledge our all to the cause of Christ, we are promised a return on our investment that is beyond measure. It makes yours and my finite *all* seem pale when compared to God's infinite *all*.

> *Then Peter said, Lo, we have left all, and followed thee.*
> *And he said unto them, Verily I say unto you, There is*
> *no man that hath left house, or parents, or brethren,*
> *or wife, or children, for the kingdom of God's sake,*
> *Who shall not receive manifold more in this present*
> *time, and in the world to come life everlasting.*
> —LUKE 18:28–30

THE CURRENCY OF DECISIVENESS

Re-read Matthew 13:44: *"Again, the kingdom of heaven is like unto treasure hid in a field; the which when a man hath found, he hideth, and for joy thereof goeth and selleth all that he hath, and buyeth that field."* Notice the absence of hesitation. Observe that there is not even a hint of waffling or procrastination. Procrastination is the natural assassin of opportunity. There is an atmosphere of decisiveness which permeates this account and so much of the Scriptures. That same decisiveness was present when Jesus was calling His disciples. One day he was walking along the shore of the Sea of Galilee and saw brothers Peter and Andrew casting their nets while fishing.

> *And he saith unto them, Follow me, and I will make you fishers of men. And they straightway left their nets, and followed him. And going on from thence, he saw other two brethren, James the son of Zebedee, and John his brother, in a ship with Zebedee their father, mending their nets; and he called them. And they immediately left the ship and their father, and followed him.*—Matthew 4:19–22

Prayer, fasting, and seeking wise counsel are indispensable in the Christian's life. Innumerable disappointments stemming from bad decisions could have been sidestepped if we had sought after and heeded godly counsel and spent time with the Lord seeking His face on the matter. So seek counsel, yes. Pray, yes. Wait on the Lord for direction, yes. But very often the issue in our lives is not that we are uncertain what God would have us to do, but that we are unwilling to act on it. Oh, for a prevailing attitude of decisiveness to obey, when the Lord clearly reveals glimpses of His will upon our hearts. Would to God we would beg Him for the courage and a mustard seed of faith to seize opportunities from Him.

The expression is not just trite, overused business vernacular; it is the reality we face as individuals, churches, parents, and in relationships. There is even a window of opportunity concerning salvation: (Isaiah 55:6, 2 Corinthians 6:2).

An Eastern proverb gives a sobering reminder of the penalty for indecision and missed opportunities, "Each day is a once in a lifetime window of opportunity." Don't be indecisive and miss yours.

PAYING THE PIPER

Europe in the middle ages was no place to be envied. The Bubonic plague, or Black Death, swept throughout the continent killing an estimated 25 million people. The plague was caused by rodents and transferred to humans. A legend arose from this non-fictional horror. In the region of Lower Saxony, Germany in a town called Hamelin, there existed a man who wore multi-colored apparel, and had a magical pipe. When he played this pipe, those who heard its melody were entranced and followed him like drones. He was hired by the townspeople to walk through the town and play his pipe in hopes that all the disease-carrying rats would follow him out of town and be eradicated. The piper did what he was contracted to do, and all the rodents followed him away as planned. When he returned to the now rodent-less town, the people of the village refused to render payment for his services. He pulled out his pipe for one final performance. Only this time it was all the children of the village that mindlessly followed him outside the city limits, never to be seen or heard from again. If the villagers were given a mulligan, I am sure they would have rather paid him with their coin than with their children.

While the account of the Pied Piper is fictional folklore, the lesson is real today. If the costs involved with procuring these currencies necessary to buy God's field are disconcerting, we should remember that the cost is higher for not buying the field. The cost for refusing to buy God's field on His terms and choosing instead to buy our field on our terms is much higher and more personal. Few people are better known in all of history for doing this very thing than Judas. Consider what it cost for him to buy his field of sinful disobedience.

> *Now this man purchased a field with the reward of iniquity; and falling headlong, he burst asunder in the midst, and all his bowels gushed out. And it was known unto all the dwellers at Jerusalem; insomuch as that field is called in their proper tongue, Aceldama, that is to say, The field of blood.*—ACTS 1:18–19

I don't know what God's field for you is, but I can tell you that it is not *Aceldama*—the field of blood. That's a high price to pay for doing your own thing. Judas is not the only one who has bellied up to the table to do so. Viewed in this light, the currency of diligence doesn't seem all that bad now. Dedication isn't so much of an imposition on our lives. Each of us will have to buy a field at a high, personal cost one way or the other. Let's look to God and make a wise, Christ-honoring choice when selecting our method of payment.

WHAT'S IN YOUR WALLET

Diligence. Discernment. Dedication. Delight. Decisiveness. All are non-negotiable tender necessary to buy the field, and all five represent very different forms of currencies. In fact, we could say that they are different than that which we are accustomed and that they are *foreign* currencies. Not foreign in the sense of a distant land far from home, but foreign in the sense of uncommon, largely unknown, or unheard of. And as a foreign currency, it should be noted that

1. We must give something of equal value in exchange to procure them.
2. The exchange rate on these currencies does not fluctuate. It is always high, for they never trade "weak" or lose their value.
3. These unique currencies can only be found in and extracted from the wallet of faith.

Unfortunately these currencies, like the $2 bill, have largely gone out of circulation in the lives of too many Christians. They are about as rare as a buffalo nickel or an Indian head penny. What's the reason for such scarcity? To exchange them, these foreign currencies require a prevailing element of faith. As Christians, praise the Lord that salvation is by faith: *"For by grace are ye saved through faith"* (Ephesians 2:8). But we are to continue in the Christian life by faith: *"(For we walk by faith, not by sight:)"* (2 Corinthians 5:7). Faith is not just something that is a one-time necessity on the day of salvation. Rather, it is a daily requirement for serving God and living a life that is pleasing to Him.

Every enduring work that has been undertaken for the glory of God had as its point of origin a Holy Spirit implanted burden in the heart of men. In order for such a work to make the transformation from a burden within one's heart to that of a blessing in the lives of others, there is the necessity of faith.

More than twenty years prior to my enrolling in Bible College, I was a student at a college in Missouri where my roommates and most of my close friends were aviation majors, all studying to be commercial airline pilots. There are many sequential ratings, or certifications, that pilots must obtain before they can fly commercially. Flight ratings such as student, sport, multi-engine, recreational, private, and instrumentation are sequential prerequisites which line the path leading to Captain-hood.

The instrumentation rating is unique and is the next certification to master after one achieves their initial private rating. Such check rides take place not in the openness of daytime but in the cover of darkness with an instructor pilot. This is because the pilot in training is flying not by sight but exclusively by the readings on the plane's instruments. Of course there is a whole world of discovery and adventure and soaring to new heights which awaits the pilot beyond that of their instrumentation rating. The point is that none of that will ever be experienced until the pilot first learns to trust his instrument readings and flies not by sight, but by faith in the direction that the gauges instruct him in.

So it is for the Christian. After being saved by faith, the next prerequisite on the checklist is this matter of learning to trust God and to live by faith. There is a whole other world awaiting the Christian—a world of discovery, adventure, and the attainment of new heights. None of that is going to come to pass, however, until we learn to trust the leading of the Holy Spirit in our lives and walk by faith. We may have a home reserved in Heaven, but until we pass this test we are like a grounded 747 out on the tarmac citing mechanical issues. Might as well ask the stewardess if she knows where you can get a Snickers bar, because you're going to be here awhile. *"But without faith it is impossible to please him: for he that cometh to God must believe that he is, and that he is a rewarder of them that diligently seek him"* (Hebrews 11:6).

Jesus Christ's return is near, and He is looking for Christians to step out in faith and buy the field. Jesus posed an arresting question that every Christian needs to take to heart:

"...*when the Son of man cometh, shall he find faith on the earth?*"
(Luke 18:8). Knowing the type of *currency* that is required to
buy the field, what's in your wallet?

Even if you're on the right track, you'll get run over if you just sit there.—**Will Rogers**

Opportunities always look bigger going than coming.
—**Anonymous**

Death is more universal than life; everyone dies but not everyone lives.—**A. Sachs**

CHAPTER SEVEN

STAY IN THE FIELD

…Go not to glean in another field, neither go from hence, but abide here.—RUTH 2:8

You've grown up with the story and even read it to children. It is a legendary tale of determination, optimism, and old fashioned "let's roll up our sleeves and get'r done." A little railroad engine was employed at a station yard to pull cars on and off the tracks. Then one fateful morning the call came in as a long train of freight cars needed to be pulled up and over a steep hill. One by one, much larger train engines were tasked to fill the work order. The excuses came rolling in: "I can't; that is too much a pull for me." "I am too busy." One by one, they all refused to pull the load.

Finally, the little switch engine was asked to pull the load up the grade and down the other side. The faith-filled response from the smallest train in the station yard that day was, "I think I can." He put himself in front of the heavy load and began to tug. At first, he moved inch by inch, but then he began to build a little momentum. As the little engine bravely puffed faster and faster, all the while he declared to himself, "I think I can, I think I can, I think I can."

As he neared the top of the hill, which had intimidated the larger engines, the little train went much slower, but continued saying, "I—think—I—can, I—think—I—can." As he drew from all available resources and mustered every bit of courage and strength, the engine did just that. He went down the other side of the grade, beaming with pride, declaring, "I thought I could, I thought I could."

THE EARLY BIRD GETS SOMETHING WAY BETTER THAN A SLIMY WORM

It was a beautiful spring day in May of 1990 in the city of Cleveland, Ohio, for the start of the Revco-Cleveland Marathon. Serious enthusiasts who desired to run the entirety of the marathon lined up at the starting line first. More recreational runners who only wanted to run a 10k lined up behind the others. Ms. Johnson, a forty-two-year-old secretary, showed up for the race intending to take part in the 10k, but she ended up running the full marathon. The Associated Press recorded: "Runner Georgene Johnson got to the starting line fifteen minutes early. The mistake cost her twenty miles and aching knees, but she said she's proud of the foul-up."[1]

She realized her error when she and four thousand or so other runners left the downtown area and headed towards the suburbs. Around the seventh or eighth mile, Georgene fortunately came up alongside a helpful runner with the good advice of slowing down, pacing herself, and dropping out once she made it to the halfway point and catching a courtesy shuttle vehicle back to the starting line.

When she reached the halfway mark, to her surprise, Georgene felt pretty good, better than she had expected. She carried on. "I got to mile 20 and it was like, well, I only have 10K left," she told the *Times*. Her finishing time was 4:04, despite never having run more than eight miles in her life. Amidst pushing herself forward at the steepest part of her twenty-six miles, she adopted the, "I think I can! I think I can!" mental fortitude. Georgene had every temptation to quit at each arduous checkpoint along the way. No one would have faulted her in the least for having done so. But no one would still be telling her incredible story if she would have.

For every right reason to stay in your field, there are dozens of causes to quit. The world is full of quitters. After years of daily, highly regimented practice, many have perfected the not-so-fine art of throwing in the towel. Most of us are good starters, but when things go off-script, and the race proves to be more drawn out and difficult than envisioned, we fail to finish. It seems that somewhere along the way there spawned a quitter's gene. Everyone is susceptible to yield and many do succumb to the impulse to quit.

Once you've gone to great lengths to consider, buy, and work the field, it seems foolish to quit—to leave the field and not finish your course. Let's look at a few of the top reasons why people who buy the field leave it:

Reason #1: *We take our eyes off Christ.*

The famed author and Nobel Prize winner Alexander Solzhenitsyn spent part of his life in a Soviet Siberian prison. At one point he was so physically weak and discouraged that he hoped for death. The hard labor, terrible conditions, and inhumane treatment had taken its toll. He knew the guards would beat him severely and probably kill him if he stopped working. He planned to expedite his death by simply ceasing his work and leaning on his shovel. But when he stopped, a fellow, caring Christian reached over with his shovel and silently drew a cross in the sand at Solzhenitsyn's feet. He then quickly erased it before the guard could see. Solzhenitsyn later recorded that that little reminder of the hope and courage found in Christ energized his entire being. He found the strength to continue because a friend cared enough to remind him to cast his eyes afresh on Christ.

Overcome the Temptation to Quit

Looking unto Jesus the author and finisher of our faith; who for the joy that was set before him endured the cross, despising the shame, and is set down at the right hand of the throne of God. For consider him that endured such contradiction of sinners against

himself, lest ye be wearied and faint in your minds.
—HEBREWS 12:2–3

Reason #2: *We focus on ourselves.*

When our eyes are no longer fixed on Christ, they naturally meander somewhere else, something else, or someone else, and hey, what better person than ourselves? This is an influential cause in the life of the average quitter. Our stumbles, let downs, disappointments, and failures are magnified when filtered through the lens of self. We become disheartened, and the next thing you know, we are hanging out in Quittersville. I am not talking about a drive-by, just in town for the weekend, or even a snowbird-type southerly migration for a couple months out of the year. Focusing on ourselves will make us a bonafide resident in this densely populated community of fellow quitters.

Overcome the Temptation to Quit

Let nothing be done through strife or vainglory; but in lowliness of mind let each esteem other better than themselves. Look not every man on his own things, but every man also on the things of others.
—PHILIPPIANS 2:3–4

Reason #3: *We are transient and soft.*

When we get to Heaven, I think there is going to be some serious ribbing taking place around the water cooler (if such is possible in Heaven). The saints of old are going to let us know how easy we had it compared to them (you know, the proverbial, they had to walk in a blinding snowstorm to and from school uphill, both ways in two feet of freezing snow). I, for one, will have to tip my hat in respectful acceptance of their claim.

Our quest for a painless life of comfort and ease has stripped us of our energy and stamina to stick it out. We don't approach our assignment with the mental toughness necessary for tenure. We have become transient and borderline nomadic. We lack a long-term "come what may I'm here to stay" mindset. When the going gets tough, we get going, going, gone. Many Christians pack it up and call it a day faster than summertime swimmers exit a public pool following the lifeguard's whistle at the first rumbling of distant thunder.

Just as someone who gets woozy and passes out at the sight of blood, we get lightheaded and faint at the mere thought of having to endure hardship, trial, or a time of testing. *"If thou faint in the day of adversity, thy strength is small"* (Proverbs 24:10). For reasons known only to Him, on occasion the Lord allows us to go back for second helpings of a plateful of adversity. *"And though the Lord give you the bread of adversity, and the water of affliction"* (Isaiah 30:20A). But we can be sure that He does have a purpose.

The following telltale signs of physical softness equate directly to the spiritual softness of Christianity today. These are actual comments that were left on Canadian Provincial Park registration sheets and comment cards by backpackers completing wilderness camping trips:

- "Trails need to be reconstructed. Please avoid building trails that go uphill."
- "Too many bugs, leeches, spiders, and spider webs. Please spray the wilderness to get rid of these pests."
- "Please pave the trails. Chair lifts need to be in some places so that we can get to wonderful views without having to hike to them."
- "The coyotes made too much noise last night and kept me awake. Please eradicate these annoying animals."
- "A small deer came into my camp and stole my jar of pickles. Can I get reimbursed? Please call…"
- "Escalators would help on steep uphill sections."
- "A McDonald's would be nice at the trailhead."
- "Too many rocks in the mountains."[2]

These complaints indicate that these people failed to grasp what it means to stay a night or two in the wilderness. They were looking for something convenient and comfortable, not a true wilderness experience. In a similar way, when we mumble, grumble, and throw in the towel, it is an indicator that we have lost sight that the Christian life is not lived at the community rec center but on the battlefield, and Heaven is there, not here.

Overcome the Temptation to Quit

Thou therefore endure hardness, as a good soldier of Jesus Christ. No man that warreth entangleth himself with the affairs of this life; that he may please him who hath chosen him to be a soldier.—2 TIMOTHY 2:3–4

Reason #4: *We are Covetous.*

A chief hindrance to staying in our field is that we fantasize about what it must be like in someone else's field. We covet the look, feel, size, location, newness, or notoriety of their field. *"And they covet fields, and take them by violence; and houses, and take them away: so they oppress a man and his house, even a man and his heritage"* (Micah 2:2). Almost every sin affecting society can be traced back to covetousness, or idolatry as the Bible calls it. St. Louis is known as *the Gateway to the West*, and marijuana is referred to as a gateway drug, but covetousness is the gateway sin.

After Jesus instructed Peter to feed His sheep, Christ told Peter that Peter would die for the faith. Peter was not crazy about the news of his demise out on the field of faith. He looked over and spotted John, *"Peter seeing him saith to Jesus, Lord, and what shall this man do? Jesus saith unto him, If I will that he tarry till I come, what is that to thee? follow thou me"* (John 21:21–22). In other words, Peter cries out to Jesus, "What about John? What exactly is the fate of the great beloved one and *his* field?" Jesus replied in effect, "Peter, that's not your concern. Don't burden yourself with such thoughts. You just focus on following Me." This is good advice for you and me as well.

Overcome the Temptation to Quit

Neither shalt thou desire thy neighbour's wife, neither shalt thou covet thy neighbour's house, his field.
—Deuteronomy 5:21a

Reason #5: *Rear-View Mirror Glances.*

When we are looking back, we are going to make an absolute train wreck of things in any attempt to move forward. Scripture attests, *"A double minded man is unstable in all his ways"* (James 1:8). Although moms have eyes in the back of their heads, the rest of us can only see in one direction at a time. Rearview mirrors are handy when fixed to the windshield of a car, but they cripple forward momentum when they dangle down from the mental recesses of our minds. It is a cumbersome, ill-advised way to go through life guided by what your mind's eye recalls.

The decision to look back was disastrous for Lot's wife, *"But his wife looked back from behind him, and she became a pillar of salt"* (Genesis 19:26). It will be no more advantageous for us. *"And Jesus said unto him, No man, having put his hand to plough, and looking back, is fit for the kingdom of God"* (Luke 9:62).

Overcome the Temptation to Quit

Let thine eyes look right on, and let thine eyelids look straight before thee…Turn not to the right hand nor to the left…—PROVERBS 4:25, 27

STAY BY THE STUFF

Sometimes we go through the motions, the routine, and at times, the drudgery of everyday life and lose sight of the fact that what we do matters and makes a difference. In these seasons where we feel small and insignificant, we would do well to remember that God rarely allows us to see all the good we are doing in service to Him. This is what the Judgment Seat of Christ will largely be for, as we are rewarded for faithfully staying in our field.

One man who hastily left his field, or more aptly, left his post, and regretted it every day for the rest of his life was John Frederick Parker. In a moment of indiscretion, JFP went MIA.

John was a Metropolitan Police Department officer in the District of Columbia in the mid 1800s. On a spring night John had been assigned security detail for the theatrical performance of, "Our American Cousin." Leading up to this evening, John's whole life had been checkered. Reprimand after reprimand had been issued to him for offenses such as, sleeping on duty, conduct unbecoming an officer, drunk while at work, and much more. But on April 14, 1865 John would receive his worst infraction yet. He and three other officers had been designated as bodyguards for President Lincoln, his wife, and two guests. During an intermission, John left his post and walked across the street to a nearby tavern to drink with a few others. Proverbs 27:8 says, *"As a bird that wandereth from her nest, so is a man that wandereth from his place."* The ill-advised time of frolic would cost more than the few bits he paid for the liquor. While he was drinking, the President he was assigned to protect was shot. Perhaps at the time he thought, what is the worst thing that could happen if I were to walk away for just awhile? I am sure that a *Presidential assassination* never surfaced his mind. JFP should have stayed in his field. So should you.

ALL SALES FINAL

I was out shopping for a gift for my wife in a small clothing store where they were having a clearance sale. As I walked through the front door, the first thing my eyes took note of was the huge sign which read, "Store Clearance—All Sales Final." I didn't give it much thought and walked on in. As I perused the sale racks, I found a lovely ladies coat that I knew she would like—*if* it was the right size. I took it to the cash register and asked, "This is a gift for my wife. If it doesn't fit, can I bring it back?" I fully expected to hear something along the lines of, "Absolutely," as if the unmistakable, "All Sales Final" sign greeting people as they entered the store did not apply to me. The unexpected response was sudden and clear, "No, all sales are final."

I stepped away from the counter, looked again at the coat, and tried to picture my dear wife in it and how it would fit her. Although the garment was discounted heavily, the price was still over a hundred dollars, and I was hesitant. After considering the purchase for a few moments, knowing that there were no refunds or exchanges, I bought the coat. (The story has a happy ending. My wife loved it and it fit her perfectly.)

In the same manner, we need a generation of Christian men, women, and young people who will step up and buy the field God has for them with the "*All Sales Final*" fortitude. No returns. No exchanges. No regrets. No leaving. No looking back. No second-guessing.

You've heard it said, "Courage is contagious. When a brave man takes a stand, the spines of others are stiffened." Such would certainly be true of Lester Roloff, a great preacher who went to be with the Lord in 1982. While he was one of the most influential preachers of his day, he also recorded a song that is a challenge to stay in your field. Within its stanzas, Roloff relays the account of the boy David, who by faith refused to run but was willing to stand against a giant. Further into the song, Roloff implores us to refuse to bow but rather take a stand, as Shadrach, Meshach and Abed-nego did. The last stanza serves as an inspiration to dare to be as Daniel and to not bow down or back away, even when the lions are in their den licking their lips. Although most junior high school language teachers might cringe at the usage of grammar in the chorus, my heart leaps and is motivated all the more to stay in my field.

> *Run if you want to, run if you will, cuz I came here to stay.*
> *If I fall down, gonna get a right up, cuz I didn't start out*
> *   to play.*
> *It's a battlefield brother, not a recreation room, It's a fight*
> *   and not a game.*
> *Run if you want to, run if you will, but I came here to stay.*"

I'm tired of running. I think I'll stay here in my field a little while longer—actually, a long while longer. How about you?

PART THREE

FINISH GOD'S CALL

You may be disappointed if you fail, but you are doomed if you don't try.—**Beverly Sills**

It is often hard to distinguish between the hard knocks in life and those of opportunity.—**Frederick Philipse**

Success is a journey, not a destination. The doing is often more important than the outcome.—**Arthur Ashe**

Luck is what happens when preparation meets opportunity.—**Lucius Annaeus Seneca**

CHAPTER EIGHT

WHEN THE FIELD IS BARREN

Although the fig tree shall not blossom, neither shall
fruit be in the vines; the labour of the olive shall fail,
and the fields shall yield no meat; the flock shall be
cut off from the fold, and there shall be no herd in the
stalls: Yet I will rejoice in the LORD, I will joy in the
God of my salvation.—HABAKKUK 3:17–18

Barren fields are heartbreaking and discouraging. Perhaps none more so than a barren mission field. Many names are well recognized for the impact on the foreign mission field, but few realize that most "successful" missionaries went through seasons of despondent barrenness. Let me share with you two such testimonies—the first from a missionary to India and the second from a missionary to South Africa.

William Carey is often called "the father of modern missions." He arrived in India in 1793 with a burden to preach the gospel of Jesus Christ to those who had never heard His name. For seven years he proclaimed the Gospel message faithfully week after week, month after month, year after year. The end result of close to a decade of prayer, preaching, witnessing, and Christian service found Carey with not even a single convert to Christ, despite his faithful labor.

Carey could easily have grown discouraged and allowed himself to return home defeated and empty-handed. But he had faith that God, in His time, would bless, and the barren field would be bountiful. Carey wrote this letter to his sisters back home in England.

> I feel as a farmer does about his crop: sometimes I think the seed is springing, and thus I hope; a little blasts all, and my hopes are gone like a cloud. They were only weeds which appeared; or if a little corn sprung up, it quickly dies, being either choked with weeds, or parched up by the sun of persecution. Yet I still hope in God, and will go forth in His strength, and make mention of His righteousness, even of His only.[1]

The second testimony is that of Robert and Mary Moffat. They labored faithfully in Bechuanaland (present day Republic of Botswana, South Africa). After a decade of service, they could not report a single convert from all of their untiring effort. The directors of their mission board began to question the wisdom of continuing the work, but the thought of leaving their post brought grief to this devoted couple. They felt sure that God was in their labors and that they would see people turn to Christ in due season.

They stayed, and for the next few years, the harvest was the same—nothing. Only prolonged, excruciating barrenness.

Then one day a friend in England sent word to the Moffats that she wanted to mail them a gift and asked what would be a blessing to them. Trusting that in time the Lord would begin to move and bless their work, Mrs. Moffat replied, "Send us a communion set; I am sure it will soon be needed."

God honored that dear woman's faith in the midst of a bleak and barren field. The Holy Spirit indeed moved upon the hearts of the villagers. Soon a little group of six converts were united to form the first church in that land. The communion set from England was delayed in the mail, but on the very day before the first commemoration of the Lord's Supper in Bechuanaland, the set arrived!

By faith, Carey fought off the overwhelming sense of discouragement and kept working tirelessly in his barren field. He would go on to establish what many would say is the greatest work in the history of modern day missions. It was not by sight, but by faith. The Moffats did much the same thing. Now it is our turn. It is our turn to work the field even when, perhaps especially when, all that is visible is barren.

I would seek unto God, and unto God would I commit my cause: Which doeth great things and unsearchable; marvellous things without number: Who giveth rain upon the earth, and sendeth waters upon the fields.—JOB 5:8–10

May we likewise realize that only God can send the rain of His blessings upon desolate works and barren fields. Let us be content to work in those fields until He does.

LAMBSQUARTER AND ROOTWORMS

Growing up on a farm in the Midwest, there was one focus in the spring—getting the crops into the field. The preparatory work of spring planting might begin as early as the prior fall. Once the previous crop was harvested, soil nutrients could be worked in the soil to give a nitrogen boost to plants the following spring. With the arrival of spring, there was much more work done to the soil with a plow, disc, harrow, and, when that was all finished, a planter. Times have changed, but in those days, Dad might have sent one of his three sons out into a field to hand-pull rogue weeds.

My dad was a good farmer. Someone could search all over and not find a harder-working individual. He was a man who not only had the physical strength to put in long hours of intense manual labor, but also the mental wherewithal to grow great yielding crops. Some seasons, he enjoyed bumper crops of harvest, but not every year. Not by a long shot. The Bible speaks of an ebb-and-flow, a changing season to all of life. *"To every thing there is a season, and a time to every purpose under the heaven…a time to plant, and a time to pluck up that which is planted…. A time to get, and a time to lose…What profit hath he that worketh in that wherein he laboureth?"* (Ecclesiastes 3:1–2, 6, 9). And there were definitely those times growing up on the farm where, despite the most diligent efforts, there was a crop failure and a resulting barren field.

The causes for barrenness were numerous—too much rain, too little rain, the temperatures were too hot and withered the plants before their fruit could bloom, or the weather was too cool not permitting soil temperatures enough warmth for crop seeds to germinate. There were other lurking factors as well. Weeds such as lambsquarter, milkweed, and giant foxtail crowded out soybeans. Insect pests, such as European corn borers, would eat away at the ears of corn, while corn rootworms would chomp away at the root system of the plant. Every farmer would confess that in any successful crop equation there are many elements in the mix that are beyond his control.

Scripture attests to this truth as well. The book of Deuteronomy speaks to the inevitability of factors largely outside of man's control: *"Thou shalt carry much seed out into the field, and shalt gather but little in; for the locust shall consume it"* (Deuteronomy 28:38). Ecclesiastes is a book of wisdom penned by the wisest man to ever live, Solomon. In chapter nine, he implores us to give our best effort in all that we do, and the following verse issues the reminder that, despite the most tireless of efforts, there are times where one's best falls short.

> *Whatsoever thy hand findeth to do, do it with thy might; for there is no work, nor device, nor knowledge, nor wisdom, in the grave, whither thou goest. I returned, and saw under the sun, that the race is not to the swift, nor the battle to the strong, neither yet bread to the wise, nor yet riches to men of understanding, nor yet favour to men of skill; but time and chance happeneth to them all.*—ECCLESIASTES 9:10–11

Along with death, the one paramount fear we all collectively harbor is failure. Failure is no respecter of gender, age, wealth, appearance, or any other demographic. Some toss and turn in their beds losing sleep over fear. Just the thought of personal failure can elevate our heart rate and bring on clammy hands.

Some of us can conceal or mask failure longer than others. For row crop farmers, however, there is nowhere to run or hide. Anyone who can't tell the difference between a cutworm and a dung beetle can at a casual glance tell if a field is experiencing crop failure or not. Barren fields know no disguise.

Despite the most carefully thought out plans and diligent labor, eventually we are likely to experience a season of barrenness in our life's work. Here are five actions to take when we find ourselves in such barrenness.

PRAY THAT YOU WILL NOT LOSE HEART

A loss of confidence and courage is the tried and true tactic of the enemy. *"And they journeyed from mount Hor by the way of the Red sea, to compass the land of Edom: and the soul of the people was much discouraged because of the way"* (Numbers 21:4).

From the launching pad of a discouraged heart, things quickly went from bad to worse for God's people. In verse five we see that they begin to be critical of authority and their leadership. *"And the people spake against God, and against Moses, Wherefore have ye brought us up out of Egypt to die in the wilderness? for there is no bread, neither is there any water; and our soul loatheth this light bread."* All of this culminating in the death of many people in verse six, *"And the LORD sent fiery serpents among the people, and they bit the people; and much people of Israel died."* Discouragement settling into the hearts of God's people became ground zero for the destruction that would follow.

The people were following Moses, and he was leading them according to the specific directions of God. Yet, the path led through the wilderness and amidst the barrenness, discouragement encroached their very souls.

If we are completely transparent, many could give personal testimony that there are seasons of life when the way is hard. Really hard. I think that writer Henry David Thoreau knew what he was talking about from personal experience when he said, "The mass of men live quiet lives of desperation." We must be careful and deliberate in protecting our spirit and guarding our heart. If not, discouragement will barge in like an uninvited wedding guest.

Missionary to abandoned children in India, Amy Carmichael, once said, "Everywhere the perpetual endeavour of the enemy of the soul is discouragement. If he can get the soul under the weather, he wins." Christian, don't let him win.

STICK TO YOUR WORK

Whether the field is bountiful or barren, stick to the work. It is not our part, nor within our power, to be successful—only faithful. Richard Cecil once was quoted as having said:

Some men will follow Christ on certain conditions—if He will not lead them through rough roads—if He will not enjoin them any painful tasks—if the sun and wind do not annoy them—if He will remit a part of His plan and order. But the true Christian, who has the spirit of Jesus, will say, as Ruth said to Naomi, *"Whither thou goest I will go,"* whatever difficulties and dangers may be in the way.[2]

Our motivation to serve God in His field must be for His glory and out of a faithful, willing heart knowing, *"All things work together for good to them that love God, to them who are the called according to his purpose"* (Romans 8:28).

If two men ever had a seemingly just cause to throw in the towel and quit the work, it would have been Abraham Lincoln and William Wilberforce. Lincoln's story is one of moving from one failure to the next until he finally reached the office of the Presidency. It is astounding and looks something like the following:

1832	Lost his job
1832	Defeated running for state legislature
1833	Failed business endeavor
1835	Sweetheart died
1837	Suffered a nervous breakdown
1838	Defeated for Speaker
1843	Defeated for nomination to Congress
1848	Lost re-nomination
1849	Rejected for Land Officer

1854   Defeated for U.S. Senate

1856   Defeated for Vice-President

1858   Defeated again for U.S. Senate

1860   Elected President of the United States [3]

Perhaps Lincoln was encouraged to continue because of one man's testimony from the other side of the pond more than a half century prior. Let me share with you a portion of Wilberforce's story and his incredible resolve to finish what he started.

William Wilberforce was a British politician in the late 1700s who championed the causes of human rights and civility across the globe. He began his political career as an independent Member of Parliament in 1780. In many respects, he was a typical British politician of his time, and there was nothing special or spectacular about his work in London. But during his early days as a statesman, he came to know Christ as his Savior, and his outlook on life and politics changed. Dramatically.

Stemming from his newfound Christian faith and keen sense of morality, Wilberforce led campaigns for causes such as the Society for Suppression of Vice, British missionary work in India, the creation of a free colony in Sierra Leone, the foundation of the Church Mission Society, and the Society for the Prevention of Cruelty to Animals. Wilberforce's most noted work began in 1787 when Granville Sharp, Hannah More, and Charles Middleton approached him. These three were activists who petitioned against England's slave trade.

Seeing the injustice in such acts, Wilberforce agreed to join them and head the parliamentary campaign against the British slave trade.

For twenty-six years, Wilberforce tirelessly fought in parliament to end Britain's involvement in the wicked practice. At times he felt he would never see victory, yet he stuck to his work, endured though pain, and continued on in the fight to the finish. In 1833 Wilberforce lay on his deathbed as the British Parliament passed the Slavery Abolition Act 1833. This act abolished slavery in most of the British Empire. Three days later William Wilberforce died.

For over a quarter of a century, Wilberforce worked hard to end slavery in Great Britain. It is difficult to imagine the opposition he faced and the trials he endured those twenty-six years. At one point he wished to quit, believing success would be forever elusive. It was then that his friend (who had been a slave trader himself prior to being saved) John Newton sent a note to encourage him to finish his life's calling. Finish he did. Let the following words of encouragement from an anonymous writer serve as a rally cry for our hearts as well.

> Keep about your work. Do not flinch because the lion roars; do not stop to stone the devil's dogs; do not fool away your time chasing the devil's rabbits...let the devil do his work; but see to it that nothing hinders you from fulfilling the work God has given you...Keep about your work...until at last you can say, "I have finished the work which Thou gavest me to do."

Christian friend: Don't flinch. Resist the urge to quit. Stick to your work. Finish.

BELIEVE THAT GOD HAS A PLAN EVEN WHEN WE DON'T UNDERSTAND IT

An account is told of a discouraged pastor who had a strange dream. He was standing on the top of a great granite rock trying to break it with a pick-ax. Hour after hour he worked with no result. The rock did not yield to his blows. At the point of exhaustion, he said, "It is useless; I will stop." A man standing by him who had watched his labors asked: "Were you not allotted this task? And if so, why are you going to abandon it?" "My work is vain. I can make no impression on the granite," said the discouraged Christian. Then the stranger solemnly replied, "That is not your task. Your duty is to pick, whether the rock yields way or not. The work is yours. The results are in other hands. Work on. Work the work."

Although God always rewards those who faithfully serve Him in His field, He seldom does so in our timing or manner. Often the reward tarries until we reach Heaven. When we cannot be shaken from the knowledge that we are doing His will, yet barrenness is all we have to show for our efforts, we need to remind ourselves that He is God, and we are not. He is the Creator, and we the creature. *"For my thoughts are not your thoughts, neither are your ways my ways, saith the LORD. For as the heavens are higher than the earth, so are my ways*

higher than your ways, and my thoughts than your thoughts"
(Isaiah 55:8–9). He has the exclusive view from above, while
we are foot soldiers with a limited line of sight.

God has a plan behind the seeming failures in our lives,
but we have to have faith that continues to serve amidst
barrenness, as did missionaries William Carey and Robert
and Mary Moffat. We must continue to trust Him and His
ways, despite great heartache and unmentionable personal
loss, as did Job. *"Though he slay me, yet will I trust in him: but
I will maintain mine own ways before him"* (Job 13:15). God
has a divine plan for setbacks. In the wake of such events,
opportunity often arrives on the scene, fashionably late, and
appearing different from what we had been anticipating and
praying for.

The story is told of a successful businessman who was
growing old and knew he needed to choose a successor to
lead his business. Instead of selecting one of his directors, or
even one of his children, he was determined to do something
different. He called all the young executives in his company
together as the following account transpires.

> It is time for me to step down and choose the next CEO.
> I have decided to choose one of you. I am going to give
> each one of you a seed today—*one very special seed. I
> want you to plant the seed, water it, and come back here
> one year from today with what you have grown from the
> seed I have given you. I will then judge the plants that you
> bring and the one I choose will be the next CEO."*

Jim was there that day and he, like the others, received a seed. He went home and excitedly told his wife of all that had taken place. She helped him get a pot, soil, and compost to plant the seed. Every day he would water it and watch to see if it had grown. Jim kept checking his seed, but nothing ever grew. Three weeks, four weeks, five weeks went by—nothing. By now, others were talking about their plants, but Jim didn't have any such plant. There was nothing visible to show for all his best labor and efforts. He felt like a failure. After six months passed, there was still nothing in Jim's pot of soil that was fertilized and watered from his own sweat and tears. By this point, everyone else in the office was boasting of his beautiful, tall plants, but he had nothing. For an entire year, Jim managed just to keep on doing what he thought was right. He kept watering and fertilizing the soil which housed the seed that he wanted to see grow.

A year finally went by and all the young executives of the company brought their plants to the CEO for inspection. On the drive into work, Jim felt sick at his stomach. It was going to be the most embarrassing moment of life.

He took his empty pot to the boardroom. When Jim arrived, he was amazed at the variety of plants grown by the other executives. They were beautiful—all shapes, sizes, and varieties of plant life graced the room. Jim put his empty pot on the floor. Many of his colleagues smirked and pointed, while others openly laughed him to scorn.

When the CEO arrived, he surveyed the room and greeted his young executives. Jim tried to disappear in the back. "My, what great plants, trees, and even flowers you have grown," said the CEO. "Today one of you will be appointed as the next Chief Executive Officer." And then, the CEO spotted Jim at the back of the room with his empty pot. He ordered the financial director to bring him to the front. Jim was terrified. His mind raced with such thoughts like, "The CEO knows I'm a failure! Now everyone will know I am a failure. Maybe he will even have me fired."

When Jim got to the front, the CEO asked everyone to sit down except Jim. He looked at Jim, and then announced to the young executives, "Behold your next Chief Executive. His name is Jim." Jim couldn't believe it. He couldn't even grow his seed. "How could he be the new CEO?" the others questioned.

Then the CEO replied, "One year ago today, I gave everyone in this room a seed. I told you to take the seed, plant it, water it, and bring it back to me today. But I gave you all boiled seeds. They were dead. It was not possible for them to grow. All of you, except Jim, have brought me trees, plants, and flowers. When you found that the seed would not grow, you substituted another seed for the one I gave you. Jim was the only one with the courage and honesty to bring me a pot with my seed in it. Therefore, he is the one who will be the new Chief Executive."[4]

Someone reading this may have been tilling the soil of his field for a great deal longer than one year, with little visible results to show for it. Even the ten years of fruitlessness on behalf of the Moffats may seem like a blink of an eye when compared to how long you have been at your task. You don't know why it is so, and neither do I, but don't overlook the mysterious ways of God. We just need to understand that God has a plan, even though we often are not privy to fully understanding it.

REJOICE IN HIM

Look again at the text included at the beginning of this chapter.

> *Although the fig tree shall not blossom, neither shall fruit be in the vines; the labour of the olive shall fail, and the fields shall yield no meat; the flock shall be cut off from the fold, and there shall be no herd in the stalls: Yet I will rejoice in the* Lord, *I will joy in the God of my salvation.*—Habakkuk 3:17–18

Even though the stalls were empty, no farm animal could be found grazing out in the fields, and harvest time was met only with failure, Habakkuk rejoiced and provided us an example for what to do when our field lies barren. The words of the Psalmist advocate a similar plea, "*Let the field be joyful, and all that is therein*" (Psalm 96:12).

In Spurgeon's daily devotional, *Morning and Evening*, he penned two devotional thoughts for each day. The text for one such day's writing was Isaiah 54, and is titled, "Sing, O Barren One." It is a humble call to rejoice though surrounded by barrenness.

> *Sing, O barren, thou that didst not bear; break forth into singing, and cry aloud, thou that didst not travail*

with child: for more are the children of the desolate
than the children of the married wife, saith the LORD.
Enlarge the place of thy tent, and let them stretch forth
the curtains of thine habitations: spare not, lengthen
thy cords, and strengthen thy stakes; —ISAIAH 54:1–2

Although we may have brought forth some fruit and have
a joyful hope that we are abiding in the vine, yet there are
times when we feel very barren. Prayer is lifeless, love is
cold, faith is weak, each grace in the garden of our heart
languishes and droops. We are like flowers in the hot
sun, desperately needing the refreshing shower. In such
a condition what are we to do? The text is addressed to
us in just such a state. "Sing, O barren one…break forth
into singing and cry aloud." But what can I sing about?
I cannot talk about the present, and even the past looks
full of barrenness. I can sing of Jesus Christ. I can talk of
visits that the Redeemer has paid to me in the past; or
if not of these, I can magnify the great love with which
He loved His people when He came from the heights of
heaven for their redemption. I will go to the cross again.
Come, my soul, you were once heavy-laden, and you lost
your burden there. Go to Calvary again. Perhaps that
very cross that gave you life may give you fruitfulness…
Sing, believer, for it will cheer your own heart and the
hearts of others who are desolate. Sing on, for although
you are presently ashamed of being barren, you will
be fruitful soon; now that God makes you hate to be
without fruit He will soon cover you with clusters. The
experience of our barrenness is painful, but the Lord's
visits are delightful. A sense of our own poverty drives

us to Christ, and that is where we need to be, for in Him our fruit is found." [5]

FINISH YOUR COURSE

If there was a man in Scripture who had every reason to quit, it was the Apostle Paul. Yet he refused to yield to such enticement. At the end of his Christ-centered life, Paul was able in good conscience to write these final words, *"I have fought a good fight, I have finished my course, I have kept the faith"* (2 Timothy 4:7). Of course Paul's motivation and example was Christ, who said, *"I have glorified thee on the earth: I have finished the work which thou gavest me to do"* (John 17:4). Jesus Christ must be our Supreme example. His life should be the pattern for our lives as well. Why are we mindful to be Christ-like in certain areas of our Christian walk but negligent in this important matter of being like Jesus in our resolve to finish our course?

BOOSTER SHOTS FOR DISCOURAGED HEARTS BEATING IN BARREN FIELDS

A booster shot is the periodical administering of an additional medicine to give a needed lift or "boost" to one's immune system. Spiritual booster shots need to be administered much more frequently. Let me share with you three booster shots to lift a downcast heart and increase the Christian's immunity to the disease of discouragement.

Courage Booster Shot #1: *Look Up*

> *Looking unto Jesus the author and finisher of our
> faith; who for the joy that was set before him endured
> the cross, despising the shame, and is set down at the
> right hand of the throne of God. For consider him
> that endured such contradiction of sinners against
> himself, lest ye be wearied and faint in your minds. Ye
> have not yet resisted unto blood, striving against sin.*
> —HEBREWS 12:2–4

When David and his men returned home to Ziklag, they
were surrounded by barrenness. Prior to David's arrival, the
Amalekites had taken all of the women and children captive.
They proceeded to burn the city to the ground. This was not
the homecoming reception David and his men had fancied. I
can only imagine the jaw-dropping speechlessness there must
have been that day in Ziklag as their eyes studied the ruins.
The emotional rollercoaster ride began shortly after, as the
speechlessness gave way to a state of shock, then to mourning,
and then ultimately to anger. As all eyes shifted towards David,
someone from deep within the angry mob yelled, "Get a rope!"
Needless to say, David was distressed—greatly distressed: *"And
David was greatly distressed; for the people spake of stoning him,
because the soul of all the people was grieved, every man for his
sons and for his daughters: but David encouraged himself in the
LORD his God"* (1 Samuel 30:6)

David was on the receiving end of the original "if looks
could kill" gaze from those around him. What did he do? He
looked upward and "encouraged himself in the Lord."

God has wired us for the mutual giving and receiving of encouragement from others around us. *"Iron sharpeneth iron; so a man sharpeneth the countenance of his friend"* (Proverbs 27:17). That's the way it should be. That's God's plan. We are aware that things don't always go as planned. Ultimately, every Christian is responsible for the overall health of his Christian walk. There are those times when a Barnabas (whose name means, "son of consolation") is nowhere to be found on the landscape of our lives. In these times, if we are to go on for God and not quit, the responsibility is on us to be found "Looking unto Jesus" and considering Him as we encourage ourselves in the Lord our God.

Courage Booster Shot #2: *Look Around*

Therefore seeing we have this ministry, as we have received mercy, we faint not.—2 CORINTHIANS 4:1

When our lives are engulfed with barrenness, we need to remember that we have been given a ministry. We need to keep our hearts encouraged to follow and fulfill that ministry. *"And say to Archippus, Take heed to the ministry which thou hast received in the Lord, that thou fulfil it"* (Colossians 4:17). We have a success-oriented mindset here in America, and we unwisely allow that thinking to drift over into ministry and church. When we don't see success and there is barrenness, we lose heart and sight of God's calling for us.

Dr. Paul Chappell, who pastors Lancaster Baptist Church in Lancaster, California, made a wise observation concerning the success syndrome in Christian work: "Ministry is not about fulfilling the 'American Dream'. It is about fulfilling the calling of God." Remember that, Christian, and take heart. God has not called you to be successful in the eyes of others or even those of your own, rather the call is to be faithful in His eyes.

Courage Booster Shot #3: *Look Ahead*

And Gideon came to Jordan, and passed over, he, and the three hundred men that were with him, faint, yet pursuing them.—JUDGES 8:4

Two chapters prior in Judges 6:11, we see Gideon in a valley threshing wheat, hiding from the Midianites. *"And there came an angel of the LORD, and sat under an oak which was in Ophrah, that pertained unto Joash the Abiezrite: and his son Gideon threshed wheat by the winepress, to hide it from the Midianites."* Threshing wheat was a work to be done out in the open on a hilltop to take advantage of the wind used to blow the chaff away from the wheat kernels. But we see Gideon in the valley by the winepress, because every time the Israelites threshed wheat out in the field, the Midianites came along and stole it from them. *"And Israel was greatly impoverished because of the Midianites"* (Judges 6:6).

Again and again, Gideon saw all that he had worked for out in the field pass right through his hands and into the hands of another. Amidst the barrenness, Gideon felt defeated and discouraged. He lost all confidence in and vision for God's calling on his life. If I were a wagering man, I would be willing to bet that Gideon was so discouraged that he was to the point of being ready to hoist the white flag high and quit. But he didn't. Don't miss that. He pressed on. In doing so, today you and I look back and remember Gideon in the same light that God viewed him when he was playing the role of the coward. Scripture records, *"And the angel of the LORD appeared unto him, and said unto him, The LORD is with thee, thou mighty man of valour"* (Judges 6:12).

It's easy to get discouraged when the field is barren, and you are searching high and low for a way out. Being called as a co-laborer in God's field was never about taking the easy path, but rather all about following the right path and staying on it. When things in your life are not going as planned and everything around you is off script and despair encroaches your spirit, cry out to God as did the Psalmist, *"My flesh and my heart faileth: but God is the strength of my heart, and my portion for ever"* (Psalm 73:26). And let us heed the counsel from Scripture to, *"let not your hearts faint, fear not, and do not tremble, neither be ye terrified because of them; For the LORD your God is he that goeth with you, to fight for you against your enemies, to save you"* (Deuteronomy 20:3–4).

FINISH IT

On October 20, 1968, by 7 PM, the sun was beginning to set and the skies darken at the Mexico City Olympics Stadium. High temperatures had cooled down, as the last of the Olympic marathon runners crossed the line and were being assisted by team doctors, coaches, teammates, family, and friends. An hour earlier, Mamo Wolde of Ethiopia had charged across the finish line, winning the twenty-six mile race, looking nearly as strong and vigorous as he'd started.

As the last few thousand spectators exited, they heard police sirens and whistles through one of the gates that entered the stadium. All attention focused on that gate, where a sole figure sporting the distinctive green and blue colors of the United Republic of Tanzania came limping into the stadium. His name was John Steven Aquari. He was the last man to finish the marathon in 1968. His leg was bandaged and bloody from a bad fall he had taken early in the race. Now, it was all he could do to limp his way around the track. The remnant of an earlier, much larger crowd stood to their feet and applauded while he completed that last lap of his race.

When he finally crossed the finish line, having completed his race, several reporters gathered around him. One man dared to ask the question that all were tempted to, "You are badly injured. Why didn't you quit? How come you didn't just give up?" Bruised and battered, a resolved Aquari said with quiet dignity, "My country did not send me five thousand miles to start this race. My country sent me to finish."

So it is with God. God didn't call us just to start a great work out in the field. He would have us to finish that which He laid upon our heart to begin. As Christians, we have all the resources of Heaven to be the finishers God would have for us to be. *"Being confident of this very thing, that he which hath begun a good work in you will perform it until the day of Jesus Christ"* (Philippians 1:6). Like the bruised and battered runner proudly wearing the colors of Tanzania all the way to the finish line, let us proudly wear the banner of our Lord out into the field and, whether bountiful or barren, stay in the field.

"And let us not be weary in well doing: for in due season we shall reap, if we faint not" (Galatians 6:9). Discouraged? Perhaps. Feeling as though you are about to faint? At times, yes. Ready to quit? No way. Not on your life.

Opportunity is often missed because we are broadcasting when we should be tuning in.—**Anonymous**

Opportunity knocked. My doorman threw him out.
—Adrienne Gisoff

Let us strive on to finish the work we are in…
—Abraham Lincoln

CHAPTER NINE

LOST YIELD OF THE FIELD

The field is wasted, the land mourneth…Be ye
ashamed…because the harvest of the field is
perished.—JOEL 1:10–11

Abandoned ghost towns from the days of the Wild West blanket sections of the southwestern United States. But not every ghost town dropped their city limit sign to zero because the gold rush ended or because of the cessation of the great railroad era. Towns such as Glenrio, New Mexico, or Two Guns, Arizona, were once vibrant communities of activity and commerce along the famed Route 66. What was the cause of death for these communities and others just like them? The advent of the interstate. I-40 to put a name with the face.

The uninhabited ruins of such towns have become monuments to the glory of what once was. It is sobering to see the decrepit state of things today in contrast with the glory of what they were. Some remnant of comfort, however small, rests in the knowledge that these towns had their day in the sun. In spite of their present obscurity and dilapidation, these places reached their potential before being cut off. We often wonder what happened to those towns. But more personally, what about people who have never peaked? Despite amazing potential and wonderful opportunities before them there was a failure to launch.

Enter Wonderland—the most amazing theme park where you will never go for a ride, have your picture taken with Wonderland characters, or cough up $9 for a lousy hamburger lunch. You will, however, find three hundred acres of half completed buildings, parking lots, and the steel skeletons of rides that could have been, should have been, and might have been, but were not. Located a short drive north of Beijing, China, Wonderland was said to be the biggest theme park in Asia. But in 1998, two years into full-scale construction, land agreements between the developers and surrounding farmers hit an insurmountable snag. They could not come to terms on a price for the adjacent fields. Since that time no progress has been made. Nada. It looks like no ride on the teacups for you.

If you search online for "China Wonderland," the results will have you scarcely believing your eyes. The photos conjure images in one's mind of a post-apocalyptic downtown Disney, complete with a Cinderella-like haunted castle as its centerpiece. It is surrounded by hundreds of acres of cornfields and shattered dreams. The root cause of this epic lies in what I have been describing throughout this book. Clearly someone did not count the cost and in the end was unwilling to buy the field. Literally. Now, the field is wasted, marked by departed joy and ruin. *"For the fields of Heshbon languish…And gladness is taken away, and joy out of the plentiful field"* (Isaiah 16:8, 10). The series of unfortunate events at Wonderland resulting in it lying in ruin is a tragedy. When much the same thing happens in the lives of God's people, it is a far greater tragedy.

LIFE ON CANNERY ROW

Cannery Row is a novel written by American author John Steinbeck. Henri is one of the characters in this book. He's known for the unique boats he constructs with such detail and intricacy that he often takes years to work on one. There's more about Henri than meets the eye. With all of his well-laid plans, painstaking efforts, and years of experience in boat construction, he has yet to finish a boat. He has not finished a single, solitary one. When the vessel is almost to the point of completion each and every time, he takes the boat entirely apart and starts all over again. Despite all the pretense and pomp, Henri has no intention of actually placing the boat in the water to set sail. Two of his friends discuss his peculiar, but by now, predictable behavior:

> Every time he gets it nearly finished, he changes it and starts all over again. I think he's nuts. Seven years on a boat!" "You don't understand. Henri loves boats, but he's afraid of the ocean. He likes boats, but supposed he finishes his boat. Once it's finished people will say, 'Why

don't you put it in the water?' Then if he puts it in the
water, he'll have to go out in it and he hates the water.
So you see, he never finishes the boat—*so he doesn't ever
have to launch it.*[1]

Cannery Row has been classified under the genre of fiction,
but this account in the book possesses a very non-fiction feel
to it. Isn't that what happens with so many of our dreams? We
make plans and tinker around with them for years, with little
to no intention of ever actually finishing them. Fear begins
to mount and, with it, the risk of failure. The uncertainty of
it all feels too great, and we eke out a meager existence and
timidly make our way through everyday life. We play things
much further on the safe side than God ever intended us to.

Rather than dealing with our fear of the water and
ultimately our fear of failure, we go through the motions
of working on *boats* that we have no intention of finishing
and setting to sail. As others have aptly put forth, "Ships are
safe in the harbor; but then again, that's not what ships were
made for."

What's the *boat* you have been puttering around with?
What has been your excuse for not finishing it? "I've been
busy." "I don't have the time." "Someone else could do it better."
"What if I fail?" "I just can't." "I'm afraid."

I have a hunch these are your excuses, not because I have
superhuman, mind-reading powers, but because of my own
experiences of making similar rationalizations. It's time to
stop saying, "I can't" and start saying, "By God's grace, I can."
It's time to stop making excuses and start making time. Finish

the boat, take it down to the water's edge, *"launch out into the deep,"* as Jesus instructed His disciples in Luke 5, and see what happens next. Maybe the boat will float. Maybe it will sink straight to the bottom. Either way, let's be honest enough to get out of the, "I'm gonna someday" mire of procrastination, and get it out on the water. If we would just let go of the fear and release it from our hands, entrusting it to God's, who knows what He might do with it?

REGRETS ONLY

In the book *Who Switched the Price Tags*, fifty people over ninety-five years old were asked one question: "If you could live your life over again, what would you do differently?" Of course many answers were received, but three common responses surfaced. People said that they would:

1. "Reflect more."
2. "Risk more."
3. "Do more things that would live on after I die."[2]

I can hardly read those replies without feeling sad. I know even those who live life all-out and expend themselves to their fullest potential for Christ might still wish that they had done more. Joshua is an example of such a person. He lived an amazing, victorious life like few others have ever known, yet at the end of his life there was still more to be done: "*Now Joshua was old and stricken in years; and the LORD said unto him, Thou art old and stricken in years, and there remaineth yet very much land to be possessed"* (Joshua 13:1). We all have a long way to go and much more to be done for God's glory.

Right or wrong, as I glance at these survey responses, I get the impression these were not likely men and women who did great things for God and only wish that they could have done more. No, I fear that these are part of the 10 percent crowd and that they were those who lived the entire length of their lives, but never come close to canvassing the breadth. These are among the many men and women whose lives were but a shell of what God had for them and left about 90 percent of His plan for their lives unfulfilled. A haunting saying comes to mind, "Unrelenting agony is the knowledge of opportunity lost; the place where the man I am comes face to face with the man I might have been." The most sobering part is that their race is run, and there is no chance for any sort of redo. Writer Hunter S. Thompson pretty much summed up my thoughts with these "pedal to the metal" words:

> Life should not be a journey to the grave with the intention of arriving safely in a pretty and well preserved body, but rather to skid in broadside in a cloud of smoke, thoroughly used up, totally worn out, and loudly proclaiming "Wow! What a Ride!"[2]

An emerging way of sending out invitations to a scheduled event or celebration is no longer the standard RSVP, but rather REGRETS ONLY. In other words, "Only respond to this invitation if you are unable to be in attendance." From the survey comments above, too many people are coming to the end of their life with ONLY REGRETS. Will Borden lived his life with no regrets while many of the rest of us wrestle from a life lived with only regrets. On account of this, the incredible harvest field God intended for us comes to naught. *"The field is wasted, the land mourneth...Be ye ashamed...because the harvest of the field is perished"* (Joel 1:10–11).

Our next breath and all the God-facilitated opportunities introduced to us have a shelf life. True, there is no expiration date stamped in ink—at least nothing visible. Make no mistake concerning the delicate and time-sensitive nature of the situation at hand. While God is timeless, ageless, and endless, His ushering in of opportunities your and my way is not. Be sure that you are a good steward of His opportunities before they—or you—expire.

You pile up enough tomorrows, and you'll find you've collected a lot of empty yesterdays.—**Professor Harold Hill**

Between the great things we cannot do and the little things we will not do, the danger is we shall do nothing.
—**Anonymous**

Of all sad words of tongue or pen, the saddest are these: It might have been.—**John Greenleaf Whitier**

I have learned that if one advances confidently in the direction of his dreams, and endeavors to live the life he has imagined, he will meet with a success unexpected in common hours.—**Henry David Thoreau**

CHAPTER TEN

A FINAL APPEAL TO BUY THE FIELD

Buy my field, I pray thee.—JEREMIAH 32:8

In the Midwest we have a retro hamburger place that is called Steak n' Shake. A few years ago, the hamburger chain ran a catchy ad campaign complete with the slogan, "Steak n' Shake: Famous for Steakburgers." They have indeed become famous for that very thing. Months or even years before those commercials aired, perhaps some executives at the food chain gathered together in some swanky destination spot. The agenda was uncomplicated and could be summed up as follows: what do we want to be famous for?

Of course that corporate boardroom scenario is completely given to this author's conjecture, but rest assured that their brand positioning of "Famous for Steakburgers" was a highly intentional move. We can learn much from their purposefulness. What is it that you want your life to be famous for? Few of us will be in a position of world-famous prominence, but we can be well known for something in our communities. Most of us will never see our name engraved in a star on the Hollywood Walk of Fame. Nonetheless, we ought to strive to be men and women of renown in our schools, neighborhoods, churches, places of work, and above all else, within the walls of our own homes. Even if we live our days on earth in relative obscurity, we can be famous in the roll call of Heaven. If such were possible (and it is), what do we want to be famous for?

Famous appears ten times within the pages of Scripture. Sometimes the people mentioned are famous for their great wickedness and other times for their great valor. Two mentions are found in the Old Testament book of Ruth. The story of Boaz and Ruth woos our thinking towards higher ground and inspires us to be known for a God-honoring legacy which will endure the passing of time.

> *Then went Boaz up to the gate, and sat him down there: and, behold, the kinsman of whom Boaz spake came by; unto whom he said, Ho, such a one! turn aside, sit down here. And he turned aside, and sat down. And he took ten men of the elders of the city, and said, Sit ye down here. And they sat down. And he said unto the kinsman, Naomi, that is come again out of the country of Moab, selleth a parcel of land, which was our brother Elimelech's: And I thought to*

advertise thee, saying, Buy it before the inhabitants, and before the elders of my people. If thou wilt redeem it, redeem it: but if thou wilt not redeem it, then tell me, that I may know: for there is none to redeem it beside thee; and I am after thee. And he said, I will redeem it. Then said Boaz, What day thou buyest the field of the hand of Naomi, thou must buy it also of Ruth the Moabitess, the wife of the dead, to raise up the name of the dead upon his inheritance. And the kinsman said, I cannot redeem it for myself, lest I mar mine own inheritance: redeem thou my right to thyself; for I cannot redeem it. Now this was the manner in former time in Israel concerning redeeming and concerning changing, for to confirm all things; a man plucked off his shoe, and gave it to his neighbour: and this was a testimony in Israel. Therefore the kinsman said unto Boaz, Buy it for thee. So he drew off his shoe. And Boaz said unto the elders, and unto all the people, Ye are witnesses this day, that I have bought all that was Elimelech's, and all that was Chilion's and Mahlon's, of the hand of Naomi. Moreover Ruth the Moabitess, the wife of Mahlon, have I purchased to be my wife, to raise up the name of the dead upon his inheritance, that the name of the dead be not cut off from among his brethren, and from the gate of his place: ye are witnesses this day. And all the people that were in the gate, and the elders, said, We are witnesses. The LORD make the woman that is come into thine house like Rachel and like Leah, which two did build the house

of Israel: and do thou worthily in Ephratah, and be
famous in Bethlehem:—RUTH 4:1–11

In these eleven monumental verses, we find the account of when Boaz took Ruth as his bride. To do so, he had to first redeem her and purchase her field from the closest kinsman. The custom of the day was that if a married man died, and he and his yet living wife had no children, the eldest brother of the deceased was the next of kin. Along with that designation, came the responsibility to take his brother's widow and support the family. If the brother was unwilling or unable to redeem the widow, tradition dictated that he (or the widow) would take off his shoe and give it to the next of kin. This gesture was symbolic of passing the baton of entitlement to the one to whom he handed the shoe. By the way, if the widow was the one to pluck off his shoe, it was also customary that she would spit in the brother's face, as a testimony for his ignominy in not stepping up and fulfilling his obligations to her.

All of this is foreign to us today. The whole process even seemed a bit dated during the time that this book was written. Verse seven describes this practice being the custom in *"former times."* What is noteworthy is that two disparate destinies were forever forged that day with the removal of the shoe from one man's foot and the placement of it into the hand of another. The line in the sand was drawn and the demarcation clear. One would go on to be famous; the other infamous. We'll revisit this climatic account in just a moment, so stay with me.

A POSITIVE SPIN ON ENTITLEMENT

In our culture the entitlement mentality seems increasingly pervasive. That is to say, many feel as though they have the right to certain privileges. Many hold to a sense of entitlement whereby society in general and the government in particular owe them a debt of gratitude or some such thing. Should this thinking persist, it is one of the social blights that have the capacity to unravel over two hundred years of socio-economic progress. This thinking will also contribute to a loss of freedom in our nation. Within the context of everyday usage in our culture, the "It's my right" argument passes right through my ears like water through a sieve. There is, however a more proper and biblical framework to view entitlement from, and the place it can be found is in the Old Testament book of Jeremiah.

> And Jeremiah said, The word of the LORD came unto me, saying, Behold, Hanameel the son of Shallum thine uncle shall come unto thee, saying, Buy thee my field that is in Anathoth: for the right of redemption is thine to buy it. So Hanameel mine uncle's son came to me in the court of the prison according to the word of the LORD, and said unto me, Buy my field, I pray thee, that is in Anathoth, which is in the country of Benjamin: for the right of inheritance is thine, and the redemption is thine; buy it for thyself. Then I knew that this was the word of the LORD. And I bought the field of Hanameel my uncle's son, that was in Anathoth,

*and weighed him the money, even seventeen shekels of
silver.*—JEREMIAH 32:6–9

For anyone who is ready to step out in faith and buy the
field, this Old Testament passage offers some final thoughts on
doing exactly that. Let's divide it down into smaller sections
that we can more easily assimilate.

The Power to Buy the Field

*Buy thee my field that is in Anathoth: for the right of
redemption is thine to buy it.*—JEREMIAH 32:7B

Although Jeremiah was in prison (a result of his preaching
an unpopular message) at the time, he was Hanameel's
first cousin and nearest relative. In their culture, it was his
responsibility and right to redeem the field. The right to refuse
to redeem the field belonged to him as well. This was no small
matter because the future and livelihood of others hinged on
his decision.

Similarly, Christians in a local church functioning as the
body of Christ have been commissioned from God to go out
into the field and impact our world. The responsibility is huge,
and the expectations are high. *"For unto whomsoever much is
given, of him shall be much required: and to whom men have
committed much, of him they will ask the more"* (Luke 12:48). As
sons of God (1 John 3:1), we have certain rights. As ambassadors
for Christ (2 Corinthians 5:20), we have been given much in
the way of responsibility from the One we represent. The right

of redemption is ours, but when push comes to shove, we too often exercise our right of refusal and in effect declare, *"Redeem thou my right to thyself; for I cannot redeem it"* (Ruth 4:6). With the blessings of sonship come privileges, expectations, and, yes, obligations to buy the field.

The Plea to Buy the Field

Buy my field, I pray thee.—JEREMIAH 32:8B

Not only did Jeremiah have the authority and power to buy the field, but there was also a heartfelt plea from the owner for him to do so. For all who will give a listening ear, that same plea rings out today as God implores us to take action and to exercise our right to buy His field.

The Peace to Buy the Field

Then I knew that this was the word of the LORD.
—JEREMIAH 32:8C

The Lord had given Jeremiah a sign beforehand by telling him that Hanameel would come and ask him to buy his field. When Hanameel did just that, Jeremiah knew this was a deal orchestrated by God.

When buying the field in our own lives, there simply has to be, "more of Thee and less of me" in it, or stated more scripturally, *"He must increase, but I must decrease"* (John 3:30). Be assured that once we commit to buy the field, trials and periods of testing will soon come our way and in such times if we do not know that we know that we know that we are following His will and not our own, odds are good we'll cave in and sell out. Like Jeremiah, we must know that the opportunity before us is from His hand and not brought about through our own posturing and scheming.

The Price to Buy to Buy the Field

> *And I bought the field…and weighed him the money,*
> *even seventeen shekels of silver.*—JEREMIAH 32:9A

At first glance, the amount of seventeen shekels doesn't seem to be a very significant amount. Yet, the price paid in this transaction was noteworthy. As an imprisoned prophet, Jeremiah would be a man of very little means. Before he was placed into prison, the money he received as part of his priestly compensation would have been almost negligible. Seventeen shekels very well could have been the extent of his personal savings and total net worth, yet the God who owns everything required Jeremiah's all.

Sound familiar? The Lord requires our heart's all as well. While God uses the sacrificial giving today of His people to advance His causes on this earth, He is never after our money, but He is in loving pursuit of our heart. Such was the case with Jesus' response to the rich young ruler in Luke 18:22, "*Now when Jesus heard these things, he said unto him, Yet lackest thou one thing: sell all that thou hast, and distribute unto the poor, and thou shalt have treasure in heaven: and come, follow me.*"

It has been my experience that when Christ has our heart, He will also have access to every other area in our life, including the checkbook.

The exchange of money is also of note because Jeremiah is the next of kin. Upon Hanameel's death, the field in Anathoth would have simply been given to Jeremiah for an inheritance as part of Hanameel's estate planning. Even so, the Lord was behind the transaction and required the exchange of money. Mind you, it was not an IOU. Hanameel did not offer his cousin the convenience of a lay-away plan or a "six months same as cash" promotion. The terms were COD (Cash On Delivery). Jeremiah weighed him the money on the spot.

There is a blight on dealings within Christendom today. Namely, some Christians, especially those in full time service for the Lord, have an unbiblical expectation to be exempt from paying full price for things and are always on the lookout for some kind of a ministerial price break. I mean, the way some of us walk around the communities in which we live and serve, the old comic strip character Sad Sack would have nothing on us. As we go about our business affairs and dealings, it's almost as though our countenance and mannerisms place those around us on Level Orange Alert—not for a terrorist threat, but for a moocher threat! I am thankful for those who have the means and heart to be an unexpected blessing to those in full-time ministry. Surely their reward which awaits them in Heaven must be sweet. But God forbid that we should get to the sad state where we expect such generosity and preferential treatment.

I don't fully understand why God required Jeremiah's all, particularly when he was next in line to receive the field as his inheritance. Even so, this account is another reminder of the steep price tag which swings suspended from God's will for every life. I remind you there is a far steeper cost incurred for not buying the field. The cost of disobedience is painfully high. Who of us is able to assign a price to regret?

The one most curious reason behind this transaction is that Jeremiah knew that in the near future all the land (including the land he was buying) would be laid to ruin and taken over by the Chaldeans. In the first five verses of this chapter, the Lord reveals to the prophet how all of Judah will fall and be overrun. Then in verses six thru nine, God instructs Jeremiah to buy the field anyway. This instruction has to be just about the most unusual, oddly-timed investment counsel ever given for all time! To our way of thinking, this would surely seem like a most opportune time to sell, not to buy.

And yet, even with God's promise of judgment on the land, He wanted to assure His people that one day they would return from their captivity. He wanted Jeremiah to buy the field as a testimony to the fact that God's judgment wouldn't last forever, that the ownership of the field would once again matter. For Jeremiah, however, to buy the field at that price and in that moment was an act of faith.

Need we be reminded that He is God and we are not? Scripture is replete with unconventional instructions from God that we could not possibly understand from our limited line of sight. If God places some out-of-the-box thinking on our hearts, we would be wise to put conventional wisdom on the shelf and simply do the work He has assigned us to do.

THE ONE WHO WOULD BECOME INFAMOUS

Let's revisit our earlier account in the book of Ruth, where two disparate legacies were forged that fateful day. A group of ten men were called together at the gates of the city to witness a transaction between two kinfolk. The writer of Scripture thought it necessary only to honor one of those men by sharing with us his name. *"Then went Boaz up to the gate, and sat him down there: and, behold, the kinsman of whom Boaz spake came by; unto whom he said, Ho, such a one! turn aside, sit down here. And he turned aside, and sat down"* (Ruth 4:1). Boaz was the one that was mentioned, but throughout the corridors of time, the other man will forever remain nameless. Not because he was a private man of discretion who preferred anonymity or to live in the shadows of public notoriety, but because his name was not worthy of receiving an honorable mentioning.

If we dig a little deeper, perhaps we would deduce that his name is subliminally encrypted in the first verse—possibly his full legal name was, *Such A. One.* We are privy to only the first name of every other character within the whole realm of Scripture, but with this individual, we have the first and last names and his middle initial as well! The point is that he obviously had a name, but because he shrank from the call of duty, it will never be known beyond his immediate family and those ten men of the city. He would never be famous, but he has become infamous. He has become notorious for his time in the spotlight where he walked away and left a good, right, and honorary deed undone.

Look at the first four verses again of Ruth 4, for in it we see that Boaz tells him, *"Naomi…selleth a parcel of land…If thou wilt redeem it, redeem it."* Mr. One promptly replied, *"I will redeem it."* Case closed. Over and out. Who's up for grabbing some pizza on the way home?

Oops, not just yet, because in the spirit of full disclosure, Boaz proceeded to read the legalese at the bottom of the contract. *"Then said Boaz, What day thou buyest the field of the hand of Naomi, thou must buy it also of Ruth the Moabitess, the wife of the dead, to raise up the name of the dead upon his inheritance"* (Ruth 4:5). Boaz reveals to him that it is not just a nice tract of land to add to the investment portfolio, but whoever gets the parcel of land also gets the young widow.

For most men, this would be a welcomed bonus, a delightful two-for-one kind of deal. Only one problem—there was already a wife and kids at home with a family photo album proudly displayed on the coffee table, school portraits lining the wall in the hallway, and a framed photo of their snorkeling expedition while on honeymoon at a timeshare on the shores of the Mediterranean Sea. Nope, this deal would not bode well with Mrs. One. What would the new girl be called around the house, Mrs. Two?

To thicken the plot and make an already tense situation even more so, any children that would come of this union would need to be written into the will, carving out more pieces from the same inheritance pie and diminishing what his current children would receive. With this catch coming to light, he pulls back from his earlier expression of enthusiasm, looks red-faced down at the ground shuffling his feet in the dirt nervously while mumbling, *"I cannot redeem it for myself, lest I mar mine own inheritance: redeem thou my right to thyself; for I cannot redeem it"* (Ruth 4:6). Twice he uttered, "I cannot redeem it." Of course, "I cannot" has a more noble, less condemning ring to it than, "I will not."

In the most unsuspecting of moments, and for the time span of a blink of an eye, Such A. One comes to the intersection of destiny and decision and of all things, locks the brakes up and does a U-turn. Case and window of opportunity closed. Forever.

Customs and protocols have changed since then for certain, but one thing has not. Buying the field always comes at a personally high price. When it comes to leaving a legacy to the generations that follow us, most Christians have made their peace with being remembered only as, John Doe, the imperceptible contemporary equivalent to *Such A. One.*

THE ONE WHO WOULD BECOME FAMOUS

While one nameless man sealed his fate that day by refusing to buy the field, Boaz secured his legacy by purchasing it. He wasn't the most likely of men to buy the field and redeem

Ruth, but he was the most loyal. He probably wasn't the most winsome, but he was the most willing. He wasn't the closest of kin, but he was the most considerate of her kindred. His story of redemption, which is a foreshadowing of the Lord Jesus Christ's redemptive work on Calvary, is told around the world today. He and Ruth are famous for the events of that unassuming day and the lineage that would come from their union. They would have a son together named Obed, who would have a son named Jesse, who would in turn have a son named David. King David. And now you know, as Radio Commentator Paul Harvey once coined, "the rest of the story." All of this birthed from one man's unexpected resolve, in the unlikeliest of settings, and in the most unsuspecting of moments, to buy the field.

EPILOGUE

THE REST OF YOUR STORY

For the last ten chapters, we have seen that we have a field
and that God's field for us is sacred. As such we must
consider, buy, work, pay for, and stay in the field—come what
may. The stories of those who did so and bought the field are
forever sealed, as are the accounts of those who did not. Our
Alpha and Omega God, Who sees the beginning from the
end (Revelation 1:8), has the knowledge that, "*all our days are
passed away in thy wrath: we spend our years as a tale that is
told*" (Psalm 90:9). In His omniscience, God knows how our
story will end, but no one else does, including you.

As we end this study, my prayer for you is that the rest of
your story will be about following God's will for your life. As a
help, I offer this closing allegory.

In the solitude of a deep, nighttime slumber, I had a sweet dream—at least I believed it was only such. I was kneeling before the throne of grace, as I heard softly whispered to me, *"Let thine eyes be on the field."* Not entirely certain what was said, I continued to bow in silent reverence, listening still, and soon the inaudible voice whispered gently again, *"Lift up your eyes, and look on the fields."* Confident of the words I heard but uncertain of what to do next, *"I was moved…to ask of [my] father a field,"* and I cried out to Him, *"What shall I do, Lord?"* It pleased Him to open my eyes and reveal more of His will for me. I then carefully *"considereth a field."* I counted the costs. I was mindful that *"fields shall be bought with money,"* and abruptly came to the conclusion that *"I cannot redeem it."* As soon as such thoughts crept through my mind, His reassuring answer was, *"Buy thee my field: for the right of redemption is thine to buy it."* My will stiffened as I refused to yield, hesitant to obey His voice and leading. I looked about and glanced at the fine fields of others around me. They appeared more fitting and more desireable. His reply, unlike my delay, was prompt. *"Neither shalt thou covet thy neighbour's field. Go not to glean in another field, neither go from hence, but abide here."* I cried aloud, *"but Your field for me is a lowly, out of the way field of such insignificance."* Just as swiftly and more sternly His words to me were, *"No. For my field…shall be holy unto the* Lord.*"*

Anxious thoughts of failure, uncertainty, and what I must leave behind consumed me, as I inquired, *"What if the fields shall yield no meat?"* But as the words flowed from my tongue, I knew that come what may, I should "*rejoice in the* L*ord, I will joy in the God of my salvation.*" My hesitancy lingered at the decision before me. My loving Father, ever patient and kind, firmly reminded me that the longer I hesitate, the greater my procrastination, then the more "*the field is wasted,*" and "*the land mourneth; because the harvest of the field is perished.*" Time was short. The opportunity was fleeting. The appointed hour had all but passed.

Amidst the tranquil silence, another statement was whispered, more softly than the first. One last petition, while there was still time. One final plea before it was too late, and all would be lost. "*Buy my field, I pray thee.*" I could delay no longer. The patient love from which those words came chipped away at my self-centered, unworthy excuses. I at long last boldly and loudly exclaimed, "*I will redeem it...and for joy thereof goeth and selleth all that [I] hath, and buyeth that field.*" Without communicating any gestures of guilt for my trifling and delay, my Father said, "*Come, my beloved, let us go forth into the field.*" From that point on, if any onlookers ever asked what became of me, and where my Father had gone, as a memorial to His grace, it was said, "*And they went out both of them into the field.*"

REFERENCES

One

1.	Samuel Butler. His translation of, *Odyssey IX*
	http://classics.mit.edu/Homer/odyssey.html

Two

1.	*Our Daily Bread*, September 5, 1984
2.	H.A. Ironside. *Illustrations of Bible Truth*. Moody Press, 1945. 37–39.

Three

1.	*Practical Bible Illustrations from Yesterday and Today.* AMG International, INC. 1996. Electronic Edition STEP Files Copyright 2005, QuickVerse.

2. John Bunyan. *The Pilgrim's Progress*. London, 1678. 246–249.

Six

1. Mark Hamby. His republication of Charles Hadden Spurgeon's, *John Ploughman's Talk*. Lamplighter Publishing, a division of Cornerstone Family Ministries, Inc. 2006, 9.
2. Ibid, 11–12.
3. Ibid, 13.

Seven

1. Kristi Umbreit. *Associated Press*, AP News Archive May 21, 1990. Last accessed on November 14, 2012. http://www.apnewsarchive.com/1990/Woman-Runs -Marathon-by-Mistake/id93316d331cb21a97b534b9 426a957222
2. Indian Peaks Wilderness Association (IPWA) website. Last accessed on November 14, 2012. http://www. indianpeakswilderness.org/IPWA_news_4_01b.htm

Eight

1. Eustace Carey, Francis Wayland, Jeremiah Chaplain, William Carey. *Memoir of William Carey, D.D.: Late Missionary to Bengal; Professor of Oriental Languages in the College of Fort William, Calculta*. London. Jackson and Walford (Google eBook)

2. Jonathan Going, J.F. Schroeder, J.M Cress. *The Christian Library: A Weekly Republication of Popular Religious Works*, Volume 8. New York. (Google eBook)

3. Lucas Morel. Compiled this comparison from the Chronology in Selected Speeches and Writings/ Lincoln by Don E. Fehrenbacher, ed., 1992. Last accessed on April 7, 2013. http://www.abrahamlincolnonline.org/lincoln/education/failures.htm

4. George Stover, Jr. *Integrity: The Last Great Battle.* Xulon Press, 2012.

5. Allistair Begg. His updated edit and revision of Charles Hadden Spurgeon's original devotional, *Morning & Evening. Crossway*, 2003.

Nine

1. John Steinbeck. *Cannery Row.* Penguin Books; Centennial Edition, 2002.

2. Anthony Campolo. *Who Switched the Price Tags*, Word Publishing, 1986.

Rob Fleshman and his wife, Michelle, have been married for more than twenty years and have four children: Tanner, Krista, Kaylee, and Kylie. The Fleshman's make their home in Deridder, Louisiana, where Rob is the Pastor of Beckwith Baptist Church.

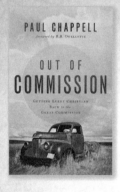

Visit us online

strivingtogether.com

wcbc.edu